North Atlantic Studies

Greenland

Nationalism and Cultural Identity in Comparative Perspective

Susanne Dybbroe and Poul Brøbech Møller, editors

Contents

Contents of next Vol.

The majority of the articles of the forthcomming vol. 3.1, fall 1991 were given as lectures at the symposium on "Local Organisation, Cultural Identity and National Integration in the North Atlantic", Oct.1991 arranged by CNS and Center for Kulturforskning, Aarhus University.
Dorais, Louis-Jacques: "Language, identity and integration in the Canadian Arctic." Jenkins, Richard: "Violence, language and politics: nationalisme in Northern Ireland and Wales." Stordahl, Vigdis: "Ethnic integration and identity management – discourses of Saami self-awareness." Thuesen, Søren: "Difference and boundary in a local community. On the formation of local associations in West Greenland." Bjørklund, Ivar: "Property in common, common property or private property: Norwegian fishery management in a Sami coastal area." Dybbroe, Susanne: "Local organisation and cultural identity in Greenland in a national perspective." Møller, Poul B.: "Images of Greenland in theory and political discourse." Mørkøre, Jógvan: Faroese Politics: "Class interests and nationalism."

VOL. 1 · NO. 2 · AARHUS 1991

North Atlantic Studies

Publishers:
SNAI-North Atlantic Publications. Distribution in cooperation with *Aarhus University Press (Aarhus Universitetsforlag),* Aarhus University, DK 8000 Aarhus C, Denmark.

Address:
SNAI-North Atlantic Publications, *Center for Nordatlantiske Studier,* Aarhus Universitet, Finlandsgade 26, DK 8200 Aarhus N, Denmark.
Phone: (45)-86-16 52 44, telefax: (45)-86-10 82 28.
Bank: Den Danske Bank, Universitetspark Afdl., Langelandsgade 177, DK 8200, Aarhus, Denmark. – Account: 4809-109348.

Subscription:
Aarhus University Press (Aarhus Universitetsforlag), Aarhus University, DK 8000 Aarhus C, Denmark. Phone: -86-19 70 33.
Postal Account: 7 41 69 54.
Subscription price, for single issues D.Kr. 80 + postage + VAT.
Booksellers price: 120 D.Kr. + VAT + postage.
By order of 10 or more copies directly from Aarhus University Press special offer: 100 D.Kr. (+ postage + VAT) pr. copy.

Financial support:
SNAI-North Atlantic Publications is a non-profit private foundation. The editors express their sincere thanks for financial support to this publication from *the foundations mentioned in the Introduction.*

Manuscripts:
North Atlantic Studies takes no responsibility for unrequested manuscripts. All manuscripts will be submitted to evaluation by two scholars selected according to the subject of the article – the examiners will be anonymous to the author.
Manuscripts should be submitted in duplicate including a one-page summary. Double space all text on quarto or A-4 paper using only one side of the page. Max. 25 pages à 2000 characters. If at all possible manuscripts should be accompanied by a disc version in IBM or Machintosh WordPerfect. Submit a short (max. 60 words) presentation of the author.
Figures and tables should be submitted ready for reproduction.

Print and lay-out:
Werks Offset, Aarhus

ISBN: 87-983424-4-4
ISSN: 0905-2984

Cover ill.:
Greenlandic Stamp still in circulation, drawings by Jens Rosing.

Introduction

Susanne Dybbroe & Poul B. Møller

This issue's collection of articles is based on papers presented at the 2nd North Atlantic Studies Conference, *Greenland – National Movement and Cultural Identity in Comparative Perspective*, October 23-26, 1989, organised by Center for North Atlantic Studies and Centre for Cultural Research at Aarhus University. The conference was one in a series of annual meetings initiated in 1988, focusing on subjects relating to culture and society in the North Atlantic (see NAS 1(1) 1989, in which appeared articles from the 1st conference on the political culture of the Faroe Islands).

With the introduction of Home Rule in Greenland in 1979, we can talk about a Greenlandic *nation*. Since the early ethnopolitical movements in the 1960s, through the emerging political party organisations leading the struggle for Home Rule in the 1970s, the key question has been a demand for *Greenlandisation*. A positive response to this demand amounts to the establishing of conditions for the construction of a true Greenlandic identity, i.e. an identity on own premises. – The particularly 'Greenlandic' presented less of a problem before Home Rule, where it was somehow an implication of the struggle against Danish political domination. Ethnopolitical symbolism abounded, yet the relation between emblems and their content remained largely undiscussed and hence undisputed. This situation is different after Home Rule, where a common cultural purpose have to be decided upon, across internal disagreements resulting from progressive differentiation and opposition of interests in the Greenlandic society. The important question now concerns: what common grounds do the Greenlandic people possess, apart from tradition, language and territory? And these dimensions, what importance do they have?

Questions of identity – what it "is", when it becomes important, how it may be studied, etc. are addressed from a variety of perspectives, including differences in regional application, focusing on processes of identity construction as well as on questions of methodology related to the study of different aspects of identity. It is our hope that the present volume will contribute to an understanding of processes and issues involved in the construction and expression of cultural identity, and that it will help delineate directions for further research.

A general note should be made concerning the articles: not all conference papers are included. We bring an article (Nuttall), however, that was not presented at the conference, but which is found particularly relevant to the present context.

Contributors to the present issue:

Inge Kleivan's analysis of the process resulting in the creation of Greenland's national symbols (flag, national anthem, national day and coat of arms) is a remarkable case of political institutionalisation effected through what amounts to a situation of *public negotiation* by way of, for instance, the media. The creation of the symbols are closely related to the modern social and political development of Greenland.

Robert Petersen discusses Greenlandic identity in terms of the relation between criteria of "Danish" resp. "Greenlandic" in different contexts and at different structural levels. A historical perspective on the changing criteria of "Greenlandic-ness" illustrates the point that the power of distinction attributed to particular aspects, e.g. language, varies with other aspects of the relation between Greenlanders and Danes.

Robert Paine goes behind the formal markers of difference between categories of Saami and proceeds to establish "Saami" in terms of a discourse of practice: "There is no one entity – 'Saami self-conscious-ness.'"... "Saami, rather, is a 'family of resemblances'" appearing only in practice. The methodological implications are examined.

Mads Fægteborg's article contains an analysis of the apparent contradiction inherent in the refusal of the Home Rule government to support Inughuit (the Thule people) claims of compensation for forced removal from their settlement, because of US military activities in Thule after WW II. The Home Rule government is caught in a dilemma, it is argued, between nationalist ideology and a pragmatic concern to keep up friendly relations with the Americans.

In this article concerning the ethnography of place, *Mark Nuttall* traces a source of individual identity in the sense of belonging and continuity acquired by the participation in hunting and the sharing with fellow villagers of a traditional relationship to the land, as reflected in present and historical use, i.e. place names.

Uffe Østergård discusses the idea of 'nation' in European political thought in the 19th century. The concern is with two opposed "nationalisms": one based on subjective criteria through the principle of personal (political) affiliation to a "cultural nation" across territorial boundaries; the other based on objective criteria through the territorial representation of all inhabitants in a region, regardless of nationality.

The article by *Tove Skutnabb-Kangas & Robert Phillipson* holds that indigenous cultures are threatened by the global hegemony of English, which serves to "legitimate, effectuate and reproduce an unequal division of power and resources between groups on the basis of language." The term 'linguicism' is used for the working of this language hierarchy which is considered to be structurally determined.

The present issue of *North Atlantic Studies* introduces a new section called *Research in Progress*. The title of the section is meant to convey the idea that preliminary works can be submitted for publication with the purpose of attracting comments from others, engaging into debate for purposes of development of an argument, etc. With respect to format: number of pages to this section should not generally exceed 10 p.

We wish to thank *Aarhus Universitets Forskningsfond, Statens Humanistiske Forskningsråd* and *Nordisk Kulturfond* for contributing the economic means to the conference and the publication. Concludingly, we wish to express our regret that the present issue has been delayed in publication and thank the authors for their cooperation and the subscribers for their patience.

Greenland's National Symbols

Inge Kleivan

ABSTRACT

The process of creating Greenland's national symbols: the national anthem, flag, national day, and coat of arms have been closely connected with Greenland's social and political development in the 20th century. Greenland's national symbols are both an expression of tradition and of change seen against the background of Greenland's ties to Denmark. Besides these four national symbols, the monarch as a national symbol, exemplified through her use of Greenland's national costume and language, is also dealt with.

Introduction

It is customary for new nations to provide themselves with a set of national symbols to the extent they do not already have them. National symbols and the traditions connected with them both signal the nation externally and strengthen national feeling internally. (Hobsbawm and Ranger, ed., 1986) They contribute to making people aware of their identity and of their responsibility for the fate of their country, and they contribute to reinforcing the belief that they will manage as a nation. After the introduction of Home Rule in Greenland in 1979, the country now has a full set of such symbols: a national anthem, a national day, a flag and a coat of arms. In addition, there are a number of other symbols which in certain specific situations can denote that someone or something is Greenlandic. In studying the individual national symbols, the process leading to precisely these symbols being used in Greenland today will be emphasised.

When Greenland is dealt with here on the same level as other new nations, it is the formal, political side of the case that is considered. Greenlanders' consciousness of having a common ethnic identity dates back to the period between 1953 and 1979, when Greenland was formally an equal part in the Danish Realm and to the period 1721 to 1953, when Greenland was a Danish colony (H. Kleivan, 1969/70; Petersen, 1976; Kjær Sørensen, 1979; Dahl, 1985; Thuesen, 1988). What will be examined here is the development in this century, when Greenland was transformed from a hunter society to a modern fishing nation, and when protection of regional special interests on the whole has become subordinated to the special interests of nation-wide political parties within the framework of a national identity.

The monarch and the national costume

Queen Margrethe II is formally the symbol of the united Realm of Denmark, i.e. Denmark, the Faroe Islands and Greenland, which in connection with Greenland means the symbol of the union between Denmark and Greenland. But she can also, in a more narrow understanding, symbolise Greenland, i.e. she can appear in different roles depending on the context. That she is Greenland's queen is signalled by her appearing in the national Greenland costume at many official occasions in Greenland, and only in Greenland. No one questions her right to wear the Greenland national costume, on the contrary, it is expected of her. The costume is a present from Greenland's political authorities and by using it in Greenland she demonstrates her respect for Greenlandic culture and identity. The Queen is popular in Greenland, although there are differences in attitude depending on age, education and political background, etc. (Lynge, 1989:11;71). This must be viewed in connection with her demonstrating her interest in Greenland in her frequent visits, 11 in all, the last one at the 10-year anniversary of Home Rule in Greenland in 1989.

The Queen's father, Frederik IX, visited Greenland three times. On his first visit as King in 1952, he and Queen Ingrid received Greenlandic costumes for themselves and their three, small princesses. On returning to Denmark, a series of colour photographs of the whole family in Greenlandic national costumes was taken, and these pictures were reproduced in great number (F. Nielsen, 1954). They hang on the walls of numerous Greenlandic homes, so people have grown accustomed to seeing the Queen in national costume from when she was a child. The first time the Queen was in Greenland was as heir to the throne in 1960. Her first meeting with Greenland took place with a big, outdoors serving of coffee and cake in Upernavik, the northernmost town in West Greenland, where she was given the official present from the Greenlandic Provincial Council: a Greenlandic national costume with short, white skin boots, kamiks, with embroidered roses and lace on the top of the long skin stockings (Hjald Carlsen, 1960). Later she has been given long red kamiks as a sign that she has married. Margrethe's mother, Queen Ingrid, appeared in 1960 in national costume with long, red kamiks; later the Greenlandic women's clubs have presented her with a pair of long, dark blue kamiks, which are considered more suitable for an elderly grandmother. Frederik IX wore an admiral's uniform then, but has also appeared in the Greenlandic national costume for men, a white cotton anorak.

Frederik IX's father, Christian X, saw his northern territories in 1921, 200 years after the arrival of the first missionary to Greenland, Hans Egede, and the beginning of Danish colonisation. It was also the first time Greenlanders could see one of their kings with their own eyes. Christian X appeared in Hussar Guard uniform with a waving plume, which made him far over two metres tall. Giving him and Queen Alexandrine Greenlandic costumes with the intention that they wear them at official occasions was apparently unthinkable. But the king did receive another important Greenlandic symbol: a fully equipped kayak, which he did not try out though. One of the other gifts was an unusually large eiderdown quilt, an example of the finest Greenlandic handicraft adapted to European taste (Grønland: Danmark i Nord, 1947).

The tradition of giving the royal family Greenlandic national costumes has continued. When the Queen's sons, Crown Prince Frederik and Prince Joachim visited Greenland for the first time in 1982, they received black kamiks from the mayor of Narsaq (Lauritzen, 1982:7).[1]

Frederik IX (1963/68, design: Viggo Bang)

costume on special occasions, she also sometimes uses the Greenlandic language symbolically in official speeches in Greenland by saying a few words in Greenlandic. In the annual New Year's speech on Danish radio and television, which is transmitted in Greenland, she also says a few words in Greenlandic and thus signals her respect for the Greenlandic language and its importance as a mark of identity (Kleivan, 1969/70; Kleivan, 1985; Petersen, 1985). The Home Rule Act of 1978 decrees that Greenlandic shall be the principal language in Greenland.[2]

Margrethe II (1973/79, design: Czeslaw Slania)

The national anthem

Greenland's national anthem, *"Nunarput utoqqarsuanngoravit"*, "Our Land, You Have Grown Old", was not written as a national anthem. Henrik Lund's poem was part of a public debate about Greenlandic society in the beginning of the 20th century. The poem was begun in 1910, the final version is from 1912, and it was first printed in 1913 in the third edition of the Greenlandic songbook (Langgård, 1987:58). The poem was originally written for the same melody the Swedish national anthem is sung to, but later on several melodies have been composed for the song, which is now always sung to the music by Jonathan Petersen, a Greenlandic composer and poet. The song expresses love and respect for the old country, but it is first and foremost an invitation to Greenlanders to take part in modern development and to believe that they can meet the challenges.[3]

William Thalbitzer, who was Reader, then Professor in Eskimology at the University of Copenhagen is lar-

Christian X (1938, design: Harald Moltke)

When the first Greenlandic stamps were printed in 1938, some of them showed Christian X wearing the headdress with a plume that he had used in Greenland. Later, stamps from Greenland have been printed with Frederik IX in a white anorak and of Queen Margrethe II in a Greenlandic women's festival costume (Kalaallit Allakkeriviat/Grønlands Postvæsen, 1988:22-27).

Just as the Queen wears the Greenlandic national

gely responsible for this song becoming the national anthem. He met Henrik Lund on one of his visits in South Greenland in 1914 and wrote enthusiastically of his poems when back in Denmark – "they have a strong, patriotic character, and have won great popularity in the southern part of the country". On the same occasion, he presented a prose translation to Danish of "*Nunarput utoqqarsuanngoravit*", which he referred to as a "patriotic song" (Thalbitzer, 1916:328-329). Later Thalbitzer wrote a new Danish translation which was sung by the students' choir when the University of Copenhagen held its memorial celebration in 1921 for the 200th anniversary of the arrival of the first missionary to Greenland, Hans Egede. In the programme, the Greenlandic text is laid out parallel with the Danish one. The song has the title, "For My Country" (Universitetets Mindefest, 1921; Thalbitzer, 1926:17-19). Thalbitzer was apparently not content with the translation, because he made a few small changes later on, on a couple of occasions (1939:19-21; 1945:33). – Several others, both Greenlanders and Danes, have tried to translate Henrik Lund's message completely, others partly to Danish with radically different results (Nielsen, 1956:40; Kjær Sørensen, 1979:58; Moses Olsen in Hjort Christiansen, 1989:10; Berthelsen/Langgård, 1983:63; Lidegaard in Folkehøjskolens sangbog, 1989: no. 199).

Later on, the song was introduced as Greenland's national anthem in Denmark. In 1933, when the International Court at the Hague recognised Denmark's rights to all of Greenland, Greenland was often the topic in Denmark, and one paper used the occasion to print "*Nunarput utoqqarsuanngoravit*", calling it Greenland's national anthem. There was even a Danish teacher who composed a melody for it. This music, together with the Greenlandic text, was printed in the Greenlandic paper *Atuagagdliutit*, with Henrik Lund's consent. At the same time, the readers were informed by the editor, Kristoffer Lynge, that the song was considered Greenland's national anthem in Denmark (Kr. L., 1933:4-5).

That there was a demand in Denmark to be able to refer to a Greenlandic national anthem was also demonstrated when Christian X celebrated his 25th anniversary as king in 1937, and a Danish song book was

printed. This pamphlet also included national anthems from Iceland, the Faroe Islands and Greenland. Henrik Lund's song, now with music by Jonathan Petersen, represented Greenland. During the Second World War as well, when Germany had occupied Denmark, and the direct connection with Greenland was broken, Greenlanders in Copenhagen sang this song on several occasions as Greenland's national anthem. Later on, it was included in many Danish songbooks with the title, "Greenland's National Anthem" with the text in Danish and sometimes with the first verse, possibly even the whole song, also printed in Greenlandic.

It was almost an accident that "*Nunarput utoqqarsuanngoravit*" was made the national anthem. It was the only modern Greenlandic poem translated into Danish in the first third of this century that was about the country. It is not really well-suited as a national anthem because it is rather dated (Langgård, 1987:67), but then, the same can be said of many other national anthems (Albertsen, 1978:76-98).

It took a while before the song was recognised as the national anthem of Greenland in Greenland. In the Greenland songbook, *Erinarsûtit*, from 1952, reprinted photographically in 1967, the song is included with the title "*Qitornat, saperase*", "Children, you can do it", as one of a series of other patriotic songs. In a discussion in Greenland's Provincial Council in 1954, it was referred to as the "so-called national anthem" (Grønlands Landsråds forhandlinger, 1954:40), which indicates that people had not accepted the idea yet. And when a prominent Greenlandic poet and cultural personality, Frederik Nielsen, wrote about Henrik Lund's poems in 1956 and quoted from "*Nunarput utoqqarsuanngoravit*", he did not refer to it as the national anthem (Nielsen, 1956:40). Nor has "*Nunarput utoqqarsuanngoravit*" been given a prominent place in the newest Greenland songbook *Erinarsuutit* from 1980. Nevertheless, it is considered the national anthem. One of the reasons Greenlanders have been able to accept it as their national anthem is that Henrik Lund was considered one of Greenland's most important poets and cultural personalities, both by his contemporaries and by later generations. In 1984 a stamp was printed in Greenland in memory of Henrik Lund (1875-1948), drawn by the Greenlandic artist Kistat Lund. Besides a portrait of Henrik Lund in an anorak against a background of a landscape, the stamp shows two music notes with the beginning of "*Nunarput utoqqarsuanngoravit*" (Kalaallit Allakkeriviat/Grønlands Postvæsen, 1988:70).

In connection with the waking of ethnic consciousness that took place among Greenlanders at the end of the 1960'ies and in particular in the 1970'ies, "*Nunarput utoqqarsuanngoravit*" met with a rival in the song "*Nuna asiilasooq*" "An Immense Country" by Jonathan Petersen. The song was originally written to the same music as the Danish national anthem, "*Det er*

Henrik Lund (1984, design: Kistat Lund)

et yndigt land", suggesting that the author had wanted it to be able to be used as a national anthem, but it did not work out that way.

Jonathan Petersen later composed the melody the song is always sung to now. The poem has only recently been translated into Danish (Berthelsen/Langgård, 1983:81). Originally it had 3 stanzas, but in the late 1940'ies Jonathan Petersen added nine more stanzas in order to describe all of Greenland, the immense country where Greenlanders have settled all along the coast. The line "For this is truly the Greenlanders' land for ever" was presumably the strongest reason for some using this song as the national anthem especially in the period when Greenlandic and Danish politicians in the Commission for Home Rule, established in 1975, debated who had the rights to Greenland's subsurface resources.

When Home Rule was effectuated on May 1, 1979, the Greenlandic party paper *Siumut partiip nipaa* celebrated the day with an entire front page with a drawing by the Greenlandic artist Anne Birgitte Hove depicting working class Greenlanders in a parade. One of them carried a little sign saying "May 1", while two others carried a large sign saying, "*kalâdlíme pigât soraiuerdlutik!*". Since they were a well-known quote from "*Nuna asiilasooq*": "For this is truly the Greenlanders' land for ever", the words were set in quotation marks.[4]

The *Siumut* Party won a majority at the first election and formed the government, Landsstyre. At the meeting of the Greenland parliament, Landsting, in the autumn of 1979, *Siumut* proposed that Greenland have its own flag, while Lars Chemnitz, the leader of the other big political party, *Atassut*, proposed the introduction of a new national anthem to mark the introduction of home rule. He suggested "*Nuna asiilasooq*", which he claimed had all the characteristics required of a national anthem: it expressed great love of Greenland and praised it beautifully; it was very popular and furthermore, there were many who already considered it the national anthem.

Since it had been mostly people with connections with *Siumut* who had used "*Nuna asiilasooq*" as a national anthem and signalled this by standing up when it was sung, this initiative can be seen as *Atassut*'s attempt to get in before *Siumut* with their proposal. The result, however, was that *Siumut* reacted by underlining its opposition to *Atassut* by sticking with "*Nunarput utoqqarsuanngoravit*".

Jonathan Motzfeldt, the chairman for *Siumut* and chairman for the Landsting and for the government, said both songs were appreciated by the population, but eventhough "*Nunarput utoqqarsuanngoravit*" had not been pointed out by any administrative or political organ, people's use of the song had made it the national anthem. He suggested awaiting expressions of opinion by the populace before returning to the matter, possibly in connection with the next spring assembly. The Landsting agreed to do this. During the discussion, Lars Emil Johansen from *Siumut* suggested considering only using the first three stanzas in "*Nunarput utoqqarsuanngoravit*" because the two last stanzas were rather out-dated.

One small public opinion study in Qasigiannguit/Christianshåb in 1980, made by students of that city yielded the conclusion that 25 preferred "*Nunarput utoqqarsuanngoravit*", 17 chose "*Nuna asiilasooq*", while 7 would rather have a new song (pl, 1980:2).

The year before Home Rule was introduced, the Greenland Landsting decided that 1979 would be the year of the song, and in that line a competition was announced for a new Home Rule song. Jonathan Motzfeldt declared explicitly at the tabling of the suggestion that "it is not our intent to find a replacement for Jonathan Petersen's national anthem. This piece is beautiful and rich in content and ought to continue to be used in future" (Grønlands Landsråds forhandlinger, autumn 1978:196). Amandus Petrussen won the competition with the song "*Asassarput nunarput*", "Our Beloved Country". It was included in the Greenland Songbook printed in 1980, where it is placed on the last page. It has a special status because not only is it the only song printed with both the new and the old orthography, but the musical notation is also included. The song does not have the status of a national anthem, however. Actually, the two old songs by Henrik Lund and Jonathan Petersen respectively are frequently both sung on the same occasions, but "*Nunarput utoqqarsuanngoravit*" still has the lead.[5]

The question of a national anthem was placed on the agenda of the meeting of the Landsråd by *Atassut* again in the spring of 1990. No decision was reached but the politicians agreed that the question could not be settled until the population had had an opportunity to express its opinion.

The national day

The idea of a Greenlandic national day was discussed publically the first time in 1942-43. Christian Vibe, the editor of the Danish language newspaper *Grønlandsposten* raised the question of national celebrations, which he envisaged would reinforce a sense of unity between Danes and Greenlanders (Red., Chr. Vibe, 1942:117). This was during the Second World War when Greenland did not have direct contact with Denmark.

Those who reacted were bilingual, *i.e.* educated Greenlanders. Hendrik Olsen from Upernavik, the northernmost town in West Greenland, suggested that Mothers' Day be celebrated, for example on February 7, "In North Greenland it is the beginning of the light time, a time when variation and change are needed in the distressing, cold and dark time of the year." (Olsen, 1942:198). He pictured a national day of celebration which would be celebrated by both Danes and Greenlanders. Peter Nielsen, then living in Qeqertarsuaq/Godhavn, interpreted the expression "Greenland's national days of celebration" as "Greenlanders' days of national celebrations". He declared that he believed his countrymen agreed with him that national feeling was an emotion so "pure and clean", as he put it, that it could not be shared jointly with a foreign people. Greenlanders were defined on the basis of ancestry. Peter Nielsen suggested February 16 as a national day of celebration with the argument that it was the day:

"when the sun, after a long period of darkness, returns to the settlements in Inglefield Fjord in the northern district of Thule" and *"all Greenlanders as a whole can see the sun reflected in their brown eyes, the sun that returns from a long journey bringing life, health and energy back to the country"* (P. Nielsen, 1943:16).

This contribution to the general debate sparked an objection from a Greenlandic reader in Nuuk, Bent Lynge, who did not approve of setting a national celebration at the returning of the sun, because it would not mean much to the people in South Greenland since they did not know the polar night. He claimed that national feeling is coupled to a people's history, therefore a national day had to be a day that meant a lot to the entire population of Greenland. Since there were no specific memorial dates in the Greenlandic forefathers' history, he recommended celebrating July 3 as a national day. This was the day Hans Egede had arrived at Greenland in 1721; it was "the founding day for Greenland's present government, enlightenment, culture and history" (B. Lynge, 1943:53). He emphasised that the day had significance for all of Greenland, for East Greenland as well, where the last converts were baptised on July 3, 1921, and also the people of Thule had felt the importance of July 3, 1721.

Only one Dane, Poul Balle, made a proposal, namely May 27, referring to a modern event with far-reaching significance. According to a Danish law concerning the administration of Greenland from May 27, 1908, two provincial councils were founded, thereby giving the Greenlandic people a voice in governing their own country.[6] This led to an increased interest in social questions, thereby strengthening a stirring national feeling, wrote Balle (Balle, 1943:52). He called the day "the Greenland Constitution Day", and although he put quotation marks around the expression himself, the comparison is not really relevant, for the Greenland Provincial Councils were primarily advisory. The suggestion was no doubt inspired by the Constitution Day celebrations in Denmark and other countries. Denmark's Constitution Day was, by the way, also a holiday in Greenland, but one of the participants in the debate noted that despite attempts to celebrate it,

it was only a copy which did not have ties with the national life of Greenland (Olsen, 1942:198).

The question of a national day of celebration was taken up again in the 1940'ies and 1950'ies. At the joint meeting of the North Greenland and South Greenland Provincial Councils in 1948, Søren Kaspersen proposed holding a millennium celebration and that the Provincial Council set a date and decide whether the day was to be celebrated as a national day in future. The source of inspiration for this proposal seemed to have been transmissions from Icelandic radio covering the annual thousand-year festivities, starting in 1874, celebrating the thousand years since the first settlement on Iceland in 874. It was emphasised during the debate that the number one thousand years was not relevant, since Greenlanders had been living in their country for a much longer period, but many of the speakers pointed out that having a day of national celebration would strengthen national consciousness. No concrete proposals were made, however, and the matter was postponed (De forenede grønlandske Landsraads Forhandlinger, 1948:193-194).

In 1952 the question arose again in the Provincial Council. The Danish chairman, Governor P.H. Lundsteen, directed the debate by asking immediately if it was to be a holiday. He found it offensive that the populace was to be gathered to think about the country and the future and then doing it by not doing anything. Therefore, he suggested repealing another holiday, or possibly decreeing half-holidays, and he pointed out Epiphany and Shrovetide as possibilities. The author of the proposal, Knud Olsen, explained that the idea was that this day mark Greenland's customs and Greenland's history and that it was to be a holiday. Then Frederik Nielsen suggested making Epiphany a half-holiday and then moving the half-holiday to July 3, thereby marking both the start of Christianity in Greenland and, as it says in the record "Denmark's possession of Greenland". He added, "in addition, the day is a real summer day". The idea of fiddling with Epiphany was not welcomed, and following a proposal by the chairman it was agreed to postpone the matter of a national holiday until the people's attitude to the matter had been investigated (Grønlands landsraads forhandlinger, 1952:265-266; F. Nielsen 1952:396).

The question was raised again in the Provincial Council in 1954, and this time a vote was held on whether a national holiday was a good idea or not. 9 vote for it, 1 against and 2 abstained. The Danish chairman abstained, but declared before the voting that he found the idea both beautiful and natural. This was a radically different attitude from the one he had taken up two years earlier, when he had not demonstrated much understanding of a national holiday as a national symbol. The chairman also underlined that adopting a national holiday would not affect Greenland's relationship with Denmark. In 1953, an amendment to the Danish constitution has been passed making Greenland an equal part of Denmark.

Frederik Lynge, who was one of the two Greenlanders elected to the Danish Parliament, the Folketing in 1953, besides being a member of the Provincial Council, mentioned the situation in Denmark, where national feelings surfaced on holidays, especially June 5, Constitution Day. He believed that most people in Greenland wanted a national holiday, they simply could not agree as to when it should be.

Only one concrete proposal was made. Jakob Nielsen from Aappilattoq, in Greenland's southernmost township Nanortalik, suggested June 21. He motivated this choice by explaining that in the south it was an old tradition to celebrate mid-summer; at this time the caplin fishing and seal hunting were over, and provisions had been laid aside for the winter. The proposal was especially interesting because June 21 is the date that actually became the national holiday many years later, but the proposal was not commented on by the members of the Provincial Council.

On the other hand, Frederik Nielsen's proposal to make July 3 a public flag day was passed unanimously (*Grønlands Landsråds forhandlinger* 1954:39-40). The next year, it was announced at the meeting of the Provincial Council that the King, in accordance with the Prime Minister's advice, had agreed to make Hans Egede Day, July 3, a regular flag day in Greenland (Grønlands Landsråds forhandlinger, 1955:22).

In this connection, the newly elected member, Jørgen Olsen, took the floor to say that he "found it ridiculous having chosen July 3 as a national holiday. Why should one nation have two national days of celebration? he asked. He found it sufficient to consider June 5, Constitution Day, the day of national celebration. When seeking equality, one should not go one's own way" it says in the record. Another member, Peter Nielsen, pointed out that July 3 had only been proclaimed a flag day, while the day of national celebration was June 5. To this the Danish chairman, P.H. Lundsteen, remarked that he assumed that June 5 would be a holiday without being a real national day. No one took the floor to speak for setting an actual Greenlandic national day despite the Provincial Council having passed a motion for one the year before (Grønlands Landsråds forhandlinger, 1955:41). The same Peter Nielsen had said in 1943 that national feeling is not something you share with foreigners but now, 12 years later, the political situation was different. The debate in Greenland's Provincial Council in 1954 and 1955 clearly demonstrated that in the years following Greenland's integration with Denmark, Greenlandic politicians had radically different views of what that entailed: from taking a continuous, Greenlandic ethnic consciousness for granted, with the cor-responding need for particular national symbols to an opinion that integration meant full equality on Danish premises.

After this, there was calm concerning the question of a national Greenlandic holiday, and meanwhile the political picture changed completely and Home Rule was introduced. The government, consisting of *Siumut* politicians, discussed the issue of a national holiday, a Home Rule day, internally. The Home Rule government was effected on May 1, 1979, but May 1 was already celebrated as the workers' international day, and therefore was less suitable as Greenland's national day, a day Greenlanders wanted all for themselves. At the assembly of the Landsting in autumn 1982, the issue was mentioned by representatives from both the two major political parties, Henrik Nielsen from *Siumut* and Peter Ostermann from *Atassut*, but it was postponed for further debate (Grønlands Landstings forhandlinger, autumn, 1982:17, 53, 57, 91). Part of the reason for wanting a Greenlandic national day was that in the summer 1982 there had been big celebrations in South Greenland on the 1000-year date for the arrival of the Norse population in Greenland, and the question had been raised "whether it was not more important to introduce a Greenlandic national day", as the spokesman for *Atassut*, Amandus Petrussen put it, when the proposal for a Greenlandic national day was set on the agenda of the Landsting in autumn 1983 by the chairman Jonathan Motzfeldt from *Siumut* and Jens Geisler, who represented the third political party, *Inuit Ataqatigiit*, which had won seats in the council then. Jens Geisler motivated the proposal by pointing out that "also in consideration of our image before the outside world, there is a need for a national day when we celebrate our nationality".

Jonathan Motzfeldt made it clear that a national day had to be a day when the Greenlandic nation "celebrated its national and cultural values in a spirit of community and of fellowship". He said Greenlanders had always been free, living under the austere but beautiful influence of Nature. And he spoke of the happiness brought by the sun and light, which their ancestors had felt and which the Greenlandic people still felt today. He proposed therefore *ullortuneq*, the longest day of the year, June 21 as the national day, intending to bind the past with the present with the future. The day would be a symbol of the freedom everyone cherished and "freedom coupled with responsibility to survive the dark, harsh and cold winters in life in a spirit of community and fellowship". Jonathan Motzfeldt called June 21 "the day everyone in this country has celebrated along the long coast from north to south and to the east from time immemorial". Strictly speaking, the tradition has probably never been as wide-spread as is indicated here. One objection is that the expression *ullortuneq*, the longest day, cannot have been relevant in areas with midnight sun, and that it was not likely that it was the custom everywhere in the areas south of the midnight sun region to keep track of precisely which day was the longest in the year until almanacs and calendars became common. But there was a tradition to build on, at any rate, as reported when the proposal for June 21 as a national day had been made the first time at the Provincial Council 29 years earlier. Another advantage with this date, as opposed to others related with the departure of the sun, was what had been mentioned earlier in connection with June 3, namely that it was a summer day and therefore outdoors arrangements would be easier to make. All three political parties in Landsting warmly supported making June 21 Greenland's national day. Neither regional nor political differences hindered their agreement. (Grønlands Landstings forhandlinger, autumn 1983 II:624-629). So Greenland got its national day symbolising the Greenlanders' close ties with nature, which is an important element in their cultural and ethnic identity.

The national day was celebrated the first time on June 21, 1985, and on this occasion Greenland's new flag was raised for the first time. Since then, the national day has been celebrated in the towns and hamlets in different ways depending on their aspirations, initiative and possibilities. Several of the following elements are included: the flags are raised, both the special Greenlandic one and the Dannebrog, everyone sings "Nunarput utoqqarsuanngoravit" and "Nuna asiilasooq", national costumes are worn, choirs and individual singers perform, music groups perform, drum dances are danced, so-called Greenlandic dances are demonstrated, dances for everyone with special emphasis on Greenlandic dances, memorial services, processions, canons are fired, demonstrations of Kayaking and traditional Greenlandic games, which the audience can join in, sports, "kaffemik" (that is, visiting neighbours by invitation to drink coffee), great communal coffee parties, communal dining with Greenlandic foods, exhibitions of Greenlandic art, cultural history exhibitions, cairn building, the annual awarding of the Home Rule government's culture award and from 1989 the Home Rule government's new award "Nersornaat".

All these events are expressions of Greenlandic culture and reinforce and maintain Greenlanders' identity as a people. Some, for example, drum dancing and Greenlandic games, are only dragged out of the closet in our days on special occasions, while others, for example, raising the flag and kaffemik are regular elements on festive occasions all year round. Only some of them have their roots back to the time before European contact, but they are all expressions of Greenlandic culture and play a role in Greenlanders' cultural self-consciousness.

The national day is not only about the past and the present, but also the future. In connection with the celebration of the first national day, the Minister for Culture and Education, Stephen Heilmann, sent a letter to all the town councils in Greenland suggesting that the main theme on the national day be the future (Heilmann, 1985).

The past years testify that some years the national day is celebrated more than other years. After the second national day celebration in Nuuk in 1986 the local newspaper, Sermitsiaq, commented that "the most spontaneous happiness was shown in the video shops – especially by the shop owners" (Sermitsiaq no. 26, 1986:32). The national day in 1989, on the other hand, was celebrated with great arrangements in Nuuk and other places as well, because the 10-year anniversary of Home Rule was celebrated at the same time.

The numerous outdoor arrangements are obviously dependent on the weather. On the national day in 1989 Narsaq township handed out free seal meat and most Narsaq families gathered in the valley Kuukasik, where they cooked their seal meat over their campfires. "The sun shone from a cloudless sky and made the day a wonderful experience" (Sermitsiaq no. 26 1989:16). The Queen landed in a flag decked Nuuk in Greenlandic national costume and was welcomed by the prime minister, Jonathan Motzfeldt, wearing a white anorak and kamiks, and thousands of festive people.

Greenland's flag

While Greenland's Landsting passed the draft for a national day in full agreement, there was no political agreement behind the decision concerning the new Greenland flag, which was used for the first time on the first national day, June 21, 1985.[7]

The Danish flag, the Dannebrog, which is red with a white cross, has been used in Greenland since colonisation's earliest days in the 18th century. The first couple of hundred years it was only used by the Royal Greenland Trade Company, the administration and the Church on their boats and on the big holidays, the King's birthday and the arrival and departure of ships. But in the 20th century, and especially from the 1940'ies, many Greenlandic families and associations bought flags and used them often, whenever there was something to celebrate. The Dannebrog became the people's flag. Danes using the Dannebrog did not prevent Greenlanders from considering it their flag, and this is why there was no hurry in getting a Greenlandic flag when Home Rule was introduced in 1979.

The first proposal that Greenland have its own flag was presented in a couple of letters to the editor in the Greenlandic press in the 1960'ies, but they were few and far between and did not instigate any discussion. The time was not yet ripe. But in the beginning of the 1970'ies the political situation had changed drastically. In 1973 a commission was established, composed of

Greenlandic politicians to discuss the possibilities of Home Rule, and the bilingual newspaper *Atagagdliutit/Grønlandsposten*, (A/G) carried the first concrete proposals for a Greenland flag, in colour: a green flag with a white cross with blue edges. The cross form was chosen to mark a union with Denmark and the other Nordic countries, which all have crosses on their flags, and the blue colour symbolised the ocean, while the green colour played on the name Greenland bears abroad. The proposal was presented by four Greenlanders and one Dane during a visit to the Faroe Islands, and it was clearly inspired by the Faroese, whose flag was in use before they got Home Rule in 1948. The Faroe Islands, along with Norway and Iceland where the Danish flag has also waved, have three-coloured flags with crosses in various combinations of red, white and blue (Bartholdy, 1986).

The proposal of a Greenlandic flag aroused great attention in Greenland, and comments and new suggestions flooded in to A/G. This made the newspaper run a vote on 11 different proposals, one of which was the Dannebrog. The finding was that the Dannebrog received the most votes, even though a majority of the voters said they wanted another flag than the Danish one. The other flags receiving many votes were also flags with crosses with red and white as the dominant colours. On the other hand, there was little interest in the green flag. Greenland's name in Greenlandic has no connotations of green, *Kalaallit Nunaat* means "the land of the Greenlanders". Only A/G readers voted and none of the Greenlandic politicians showed any interest in looking into the matter at that point in time.

Not until after the introduction of Home Rule had been celebrated with a profusion of Dannebrog flags on May 1, 1979, was the question of a special flag for Greenland raised in the Landsting in the autumn of the same year by Henrik Nielsen from *Siumut*. In early 1980, a public competition was announced about what the new flag for Greenland ought to look like, but it was quite a while before a decision was reached. Hundreds of suggestions were sent in, mostly from Greenland, but many came from Denmark and a few from other countries.

While the decision was delayed, people still flew the Danish flag. Few consciously avoided flying a flag or demonstratively flew their own private proposals for a flag for Greenland. Some pressure was applied on Greenlandic politicians in Denmark and in the other Nordic countries in connection with meetings and sports events, where Greenland's flag was expected to indicate that representatives from Greenland were taking part, but in light of the close affinity many Greenlanders felt for the Dannebrog, the politicians were not particularly interested in a decision. One prominent member of *Siumut*, Lars Emil Johansen, said on several occasions that the Dannebrog was the most beautiful flag in the world. The committee responsible for the new flag, which comprised representatives from *Siumut* and *Atassut* and later on also from *Inuit Ataqatigiit*, and which had artistic and heraldic experts associated with it, was not satisfied with the proposals they had received. Some Greenlandic artists were encouraged to make suggestions for a flag, which was not to be a cross flag, while the committee itself would draw up a suggestion for a flag with a cross.

In February 1985 the Landsting had two proposals to choose between: a green flag with a white cross and the red and white flag that is Greenland's flag today and which was drawn by the Greenlandic artist Thue Christiansen. The flag is divided into two halves, a red field below and a white one on top. A large sphere is placed in the middle along the centre axis, displaced towards the flagpole, the red half on the white field, the white half on the red field. The vote was secret, the results were 11-14. Probably the voting was based on political affiliation, because *Atassut* had supported the first proposal, while *Siumut* and *Inuit Ataqatigiit* had supported the latter. Various politicians had indicated over the years that they wanted a plebiscite on which flag ought to be Greenland's, but when it came to the point, they refrained, saying that they did not want to cause divisions among the populace. For a while, however, the flag was more of a divisive factor than a unifying one.

Negative reactions were prompt, not only from *Atassut* supporters, but also from other people. Many were dissatisfied because the plebiscite was not held, and many indicated that they would have preferred a flag with a cross, one which resembled the Dannebrog as much as possible, then again, many even wanted to keep the Dannebrog. No one spoke out on behalf of the green flag with a cross. Then it turned out that both flags were in use in other places. The green flag with a cross was identical with the flag for the independence party in Puerto Rico, and the red and white flag with a sphere was identical with the banner used by a rowing section of a Danish athletics club in Hjorthøj Egå. This did not prevent the same drawing being used as a national flag, but it did increase discontent with the flag the Landsting had chosen. *Atassut* tried to bring the matter up again, but the parties composing a majority in Landsting refused. *Atassut* members walked out in protest, and a considerable number of signatures were collected in petitions. Otto Steenholt, the chairman for *Atassut* and one of the two Greenlandic members of the Folketing in Denmark, saw to it that the matter was dealt with in the special committee for Greenland in the Folketing. But the Folketing took the advice of Landsting and unanimously voted to grant a special Greenland flag. The Folketing had nothing to do with what the flag looked like. Then the Landsting passed a law concerning Greenland's flag on June 11, 1985, saying, among other things, that

Greenland's flag must be treated with respect. It said nothing about the flag's appearance, so all Greenlandic parties could vote for it.

The Greenlandic politicians had chosen a flag that was decisively different from all the Nordic flags. Greenland's having affiliations not only with Nordic countries, but also with other Inuits played a small role in the debate, but was mentioned though, when explaining why the Greenland flag was not automatically one with a cross. The decision by Greenlandic politicians sitting in the Landsting, both from *Siumut* and *Inuit Ataqatigiit* parties to select a flag so different from the Nordic flags is not necessarily directed specifically towards Denmark and the Nordic countries. In the days immediately before the decision concerning the flag, the politicians and supporters of the same two parties celebrated Greenland's withdrawal from the European Economic Community, emphasising the increase in independence Greenland had won thereby. As early as in 1976 Lars Emil Johansen had hinted at the solution that actually was adopted: "It is an idea that suggests itself that if we are to have a flag it ought to express our uniqueness in Greenland rather than our connections with the outside world. Our associations might be symbolised in the colours in the flag" (Grønlands fremtid, 1976:64-65).

The colours of Greenland's flag are precisely the same colours as in the Danish flag: red and white. The flag does not symbolise certain historic events, as is the case with some flags, or include specific ethnic, cultural symbols, as can be found for example, in *Inuit Ataqatigiit*'s party banner, which has a white harpoon point and a woman's knife, *ulu*, on a red field in the top corner closest to the pole.[8] Greenland's flag, like the national day, symbolises Greenlanders' close affinity with nature: like a red ball, the sun hovers over the snow-clad mountains, the same sun that paints the ocean red.

The official flag days were settled in a decree on June 21, 1985 and did not involve any great breach of tradition. Church festivals, the Queen's birthday and those of her family, and U.N. day, October 24 are still official flag-flying days. The flag is still hoisted on four historic memorial days Greenland has in common with Denmark: June 15 (1219, Valdemar's Day, when the Dannebrog is supposed to have fallen from the hea-

The Greenlandic flag (1989, design: C. Achton Friis)

vens, and 1920, the re-unification of southern Jutland with Denmark), June 5 (1849, Denmark's Constitution Day, and 1953, when Greenland was included in the Constitution), April 9, when the flag is half-masted until 12 o'clock (1940, when Denmark was occupied by Germany and direct contact with Greenland was interrupted) and May 5 (1945, Denmark's liberation, when connections with Greenland were re-established). Furthermore, the following days with special importance for Greenland are flag-flying days in Greenland, but not in Denmark: July 3 (1721, Hans Egede's arrival in Greenland), May 1 (1979, the introduction of Home Rule in Greenland and 1890, the international labourers' day) and June 21 (1985, Greenland's national day). Finally the decree dictates that flags may be flown on other days than the afore-mentioned and flags are hoisted on many other occasions when people want to signal they have something to celebrate.

After Greenland's new flag was officially introduced, the public discussion abated. Danish officials in Greenland still have to use the Dannebrog, and private people are allowed to use it as well. This meant that the many disgruntled people had an alternative. The two red-and-white flags wave side by side on festive occasions, but more and more people adopt the Greenland flag. This does not connote that the many people still using the Danish flag want to express their lack of confidence in the Home Rule government, but for many Greenlanders the Dannebrog still represents the flag they have always considered their own.

Greenland's flag, together with the Dannebrog, was replicated on a Greenlandic stamp in 1986 to mark Greenland's Home Rule taking over the Postal Service in Greenland, but in connection with the 10th anniversary of Home Rule in 1989 a stamp was printed where only Greenland's flag waves over the red houses with snow-clad mountains in the background. When the Greenlandic Christmas stamp was printed later the same year though, it included both the Greenlandic and Danish flags. The artist responsible for the stamp from 1986 and the Christmas stamp from 1989 was

The Danish and the Greenlandic flag (1986, design: Thue Christiansen)

Thue Christiansen, the man who had designed the Greenlandic flag.

In 1987 a league was started, *Erfalasorput* or "Our Flag", which aspired to strengthen love of Greenland and the new Greenlandic flag.

A public opinion study from 1989 showed that 56% preferred the Greenlandic flag, 17% the Dannebrog, 20% preferred another flag and 7% answered "don't know". The youngest individuals were the most positive towards the new flag, the oldest ones the most negative, but it was clear that four years after its introduction Greenland's flag was accepted by a majority of the population (Sermitsiaq nr. 18, 1990, p. 11).

Greenland's Coat of Arms

Greenland's coat of arms is a silver polar bear with a red tongue on a blue background. The bear is sitting on its hind legs and waving its paws in the air. It faces left and the left forepaw is highest up. It is the same polar bear that appears on the shield of arms used by state institutions in Greenland, but here it has its right paw raised, as was the case on earlier shields of arms with a sitting bear. Furthermore, there is a crown at the top of the state's coat of arms.

Greenland's new coat of arms was introduced by the Ministry for Greenland in a decree no. 134 of March 12, 1987. It was designed by the state's consultant in heraldry, Georg Bartholdy, with help from the royal coat of arms painter, Aage Wulff, after representatives from the various political parties in Greenland's Landsting had agreed in the autumn of 1985 that the coat of arms of Greenland would be a polar bear.

There is a long tradition for a polar bear symbolising Greenland. The polar bear figured in Frederik III's royal coat of arms from 1666, but might have been used a little earlier as well. The bear was also replicated on coins and seals. At that time, there were no Danes in Greenland, but the Crown wanted to manifest that Greenland belonged to it. The polar bear disappeared from royal coat of arms later, but was included again by Frederik VI in 1820, and since then there has been a silver polar bear in various versions on a blue background (Bjerg, 1974; Bjerg, 1975; Haxthausen, 1973: 302).

Since 1776, the polar bear has also been used in the Royal Greenland Trade Company's (KGH) seal. Over the years, three different versions of a sitting/standing bear have existed. The last alteration was in 1958 (Bjerg, 1974; Bjerg, 1975). In 1985 Greenland's Home Rule government took over the Royal Greenland Trade Monopoly's production and export sector, while the other sectors: retail, the postal service, etc. were taken over the following year. In this connection, *Kalaallit Niuerfiat* (KNI), Greenland's Trade Company, started using a new trademark in its shops. It is quite

different from the earlier one, but the polar bear is still there. It shows two polar bears, one in front of the other, standing in profile, and there is also a star on the blue background, which is framed by a white and a blue circle (Sermitsiaq 1986 no. 1:1). The trademark was designed by Thue Christiansen.

Greenlands Postal Service still uses the old bear from 1958. Probably the reason is that all signs were replaced when the postal service was taken over by the Home Rule government in 1986. That meant removing the crown in the coat of arms with the bear and the Danish text "Greenland's Postal Service" was replaced with the equivalent Greenlandic "*Kalaallit Allakkeriviat*". When the first Greenlandic stamps were issued in 1938, one of the motifs was of a polar bear walking on the ice. Later, on several occasions, Greenlandic stamps depicting a polar bear have been printed (Kalaallit Allakkeriviat/Grønlands Postvæsen, 1988:30-31). In connection with the 10th anniversary of Home Rule in 1989 a stamp was printed with the new coat of arms.

While Greenlandic stamps still continue to show glimpses of Greenland's culture and scenery and most often are drawn by Greenlandic artists, there is no longer Greenlandic money. But from 1803 to 1967, special Greenlandic bills and some coins were used as well, and many of these were decorated with a polar bear (Flensborg, 1970; Holm, 1957; Christiansen, 1962).

When the final design of Greenland's new coat of arms was made public it contained a surprise. The bear had a raised left forepaw, while it had always formerly had raised its right paw. The right hand symbolises power and strength, and the Greenlandic trade union *Sulinermik Inuutissssarsiuteqartut Kattuffiat* (S.I.K.) has followed European patterns and uses a raised right fist as its logo. Why, then, a bear with its left forepaw ready to strike? "It is old Greenlandic wisdom that the polar bear strikes with its left paw" was the explanation at the presentation of Greenland's new coat of arms (Grønlands Hjemmestyre, 1988:144). "The state has been fonder of tradition

Greenland's coat of arms (1989, design: C. Achton Friis)

than biology" it was added. As mentioned earlier, the state's newly designed bear still has its right paw in the air.

Considering how many accounts there are of polar bears in literature on the Arctic, it is rather surprising that this observation apparently has only been made by Greenlanders and other Inuit (Cf. Saladin d'Anglure 1990:190). Even the renowned polar bear expert Thor Larsen is not vouch for this claim, because he writes that

> "The Thule Eskimos from Greenland *claimed* that polar bears were only able to strike with their left paw. Therefore, it was less dangerous for the hunter to approach the animal from the left" (Larsen, 1978:10). (my italics)

In the opus on Greenland's fauna, *Grønlands Fauna*, which was printed in Danish in 1981 and in translation to Greenlandic in 1985, the zoologist Christian Vibe writes: " The Eskimos report that the polar bear always strikes with its left paw when it attacks" (Vibe, 1981:385). There is not doubt that Vibe is referring to the *inughuit*/Polar Eskimos, but nevertheless it was translated into Greenlandic with *"kalaallit oqaatigisarpaat"*, i.e. "Greenlanders say" (Vibe 1985:385). It this simply a mistake in translation, or has the translator written *kalaallit* to indicate that it is also general knowledge in West Greenland?

If many people in West Greenland are of the opinion that the polar bears strikes with its left paw, this knowledge may derived from the *inughuit* in recent times anyway. Polar bears are rare guests in West Greenland, except for the southern part of the coast where the ice sometimes brings polar bears with it from the east coast. For *inughuit* in North Greenland a bear hunt is not a rarity. One of the sources of knowledge on the polar bear's behaviour is a Greenland schoolbook *Thulep uumasui pingaarnerit* "The Most Important Animals in Thule", which was published a few years before "The Fauna of Greenland". Here Peter Jensen, originally from West Greenland, but for many years a catechist in Northern Greenland, tells how a polar bear positions itself beside a seal's breathing hole and the minute the seal turns up to breathe, the bear strikes it on the head with its left paw, so the head is smashed. (Jensen, 1979:56).

However, the central point in relation with Greenland's new coat of arms is not whether or not the polar bear really is left-handed.[9] The main point is that Greenlanders still keep up the tradition of letting the polar bear symbolise Greenland, at the same having clearly marked that the Greenlandic bear is different from the Danish one. It is also important that this view is associated with the world's most northern, highly-qualified hunters, who compose part of the Greenlandic nation, for hunting is an important element in the ethnic and cultural identity of the Greenlanders.

A few years after Greenland's new coat of arms was a reality, a Greenlandic award was founded, *"Nersornaat"* in connection with the 10th anniversary of Greenland's Home Rule on May 1, 1989. On the front is the inscription *"Kalaallit Nunaat"*, "Greenland", and a seated bear with its left side facing out and its left paw highest up, but on the medal the paw is not raised to strike. The polar bear sits calmly and in a dignified manner with a straight back. On the back of the medal are the words *"Nersornaat"*, "award", and under them a yellow Arctic Poppy. The Greenlandic flag is woven into the red-and-white medal ribbon. The silver medal is made of silver from Maarmorilik mine on the northern part of the west coast. In the long run, they hope to be able to make the gold medal out of Greenlandic gold as well. The medal was designed by the Greenlandic artist Jens Rosing.

Choosing the polar bear as the motif was what could be expected. That the medal is also decorated with a flower marks Greenland's being not only snow and ice, but that the choice fell on the Arctic Poppy *Papaver radicatum*, in Greenlandic *sungaartorsuaq*, "the big yellow one" (Feiber, Fredskild and Holt, 1984: no. 42; Foersom, Kapel and Svarre, 1982:111) was not a matter of course. Through the years another flower has earned the nickname Greenland's national flower: the Broad-leafed Willow-herb, *Chamaenerion latifolium*, in Greenlandic *paannaaq* or *aappaluttorsuit* "the big red one" or *niviarsiaq* "maiden" (Feilberg, Fredskild and Holt 1984: no. 38; Foersom, Kapel and Svarre 1982:114). The Broad-leafed Willow-herb was not, however, suitable as a symbol on Greenland's Home Rule medal, because the Greenlandic political party *Siumut* had used this flowers as its symbol for quite a while.[10] The two flowers, the Arctic Poppy and the Broad-leafed Willow-herb, are both quite common over all of Greenland and their flowers are precisely as their Greenlandic names indicate, unusually big and beautiful by Greenlandic standards. The same year the Greenlandic honor was founded, Greenland's Postal Service printed two stamps with flower motifs for the first time in its 51-year history. The one depicted polar cotton-grass, *Eriophorum scheuchzeri*, in Greenlandic *ukaliusaq*, while the other was of the Arctic Poppy.

Conclusion

Many Greenlanders have taken part in the discussions in connection with the establishment of Greenland's national symbols, both in private and in political organs, but also in the mass media, primarily in the printed Greenlandic press, which has a long tradition of people airing their opinions here.

A nation defines itself in relation to other nations in terms of its national symbols. When it is the case, as it is here, that one nation has had, and still has, a close connection with a certain other nation, it is natural that this will be the nation one defines oneself in relation to. Greenland's national symbols represent both continuity and change in relation to Denmark. This fact is symbolised clearly in Greenland's new flag, which uses the same colours as the Dannebrog, but the design is very different. The same can be said of Greenland's coat of arms, which still uses a polar bear, which Denmark has used for centuries as a symbol of Greenland, but the Greenlandic polar bear has its left paw raised whereas the Danish one has its right paw raised.

One element the three national symbols: the flag, coat of arms and the national day, share is that they express Greenlanders' close ties with nature. This element is also a part of the national anthem about the ancient country, which has bestowed its riches upon its children, *kalaallit*, the Greenlanders, but the song is mainly the expression of the author's thoughts concerning the need for development in the beginning of the 20th century. It is not unthinkable then, that the recent attempt to replace this national anthem with a new one will succeed.

Greenlanders got a national anthem before they felt the need of one themselves because the Danes needed to be able to refer to a Greenlandic national anthem. The decision concerning the flag was partially taken in answer to the rest of the world's expectations that Greenland ought to have its own flag, but both these national symbols would have been created at some point anyway.

Whereas the first discussions about a national day reflected regional interests, but ended in complete agreement, the political frictions came into the open in discussions about the national song and flag. Although a political majority in Greenland's Landsting made the decision on these questions, these issues did not lead to any serious divisions among the population in the long run because Greenlandic society is tolerant enough to make room for an alternative flag and an alternative song, both of which have well-established roots in Greenland.

4.) We want very much to follow the course of a mature people. We are longing to use freedom of speech and press!

5.) There is not at all the slightest reason for holding back. Greenlanders, stand up on your feet, forward! It is well worth to live as men. Show that you can think for yourselves!"

(English prose translation of *Nunarput utoqqarsuanngoravit* in Frederiksen, 1952:658).

4. This might be a case of recycling. The drawing is dated 1987.

5. The Danish song to the king, *Kong Kristian stod ved højen mast* has not been translated into Greenlandic, but among the songs of tribute written to the king in Greenlandic is one by Hans Hansen to the music the Danish song to the king is sung to: *atarqivātit, kúnge-â* "They honour you, oh king". It is included in the various editions of the Greenland song book from 1913-1967, but not in the latest one from 1980. The Danish national anthem *Det er et yndigt land* has not been translated into Greenlandic, as far as I know. The closest choice for a common national anthem in Greenlandic for both Greenlanders and Danes would have been Jonathan Petersen's *Erfalasorput* "Our flag", which praises the red and white cross flag that Greenlanders and Danes own jointly. The song used to be very popular, but after many people have begun using the special Greenland flag it no longer has the same significance. (Danish translation: Berthelsen/Langgård, 1983:83-84)

6. Or more correctly, half of the adult population of Greenland, because Greenlandic women did not get the franchise until 1948.

7. The background for Greenlanders' close affinity to the Danish flag and a more detailed account of the debate in connection with Greenland's new flag can be found in I. Kleivan 1988.

8. Concerning the harpoon and ulu as ethno-political symbols, see Rasmussen 1983:278-282).

9. In a guide to polar bear hunting in a Greenlandic textbook on hunting from 1922 for South Greenland it says about hunting polar bears from a kayak, "Some lance a bear by placing themselves so that they have it to their left and try to hit it in the heart, others prefer to have the bear on their right... If your lance sticks in the bear, you will soon see how agile it is. It will grab the lance with its claws on its left paw and remove it as if it had a hand " (Kleist, 1922:36-37; Kleist, 1971:65-66). Is this proof that the polar bear is left-handed, or is it rather the case that the swimming bear must use its strongest paw, the right one, to hold itself up? The polar bear in the new Greenland coat of arms is certainly not naturalistic on all points: it has a long, red tongue, which makes it look lively and dangerous, but in reality the polar bear has a small blue-purple tongue. Therefore in the latest sketch for a polar bear for KGH's coat of arms (1958), it was depicted with wide-open, threatening jaws (sic. 1959:8-9).

10. When the *Siumut* party revived the party newspaper, *Siumut*, in 1987, its name was changed to *Niviarsiaq Siumup avisia* to indicate that the party wanted to change its style. (Johansen, 1987:2-3) The heading shows three red flowers of the Broadleafed Willow-herb, *niviarsiaq*.

Notes

1. On ethnic and social boundaries marked through the use of clothes in Greenland see Rasmussen 1983.

2. "(1) Greenlandic shall be the principal language. Danish must be thoroughly taught. (2) Either language may be used for official purposes" (The Greenland Home Rule Act, Chapter 2, section 9 – published in English translation in Foighel 1980:16).

3. " 1.) Our country, when you grew very old, your hair was crowned with white hair. You carried steadfast your children in your arms and gave them what belonged to your coast land.

   2.) We who grew up with you as an immature people, as small children, we want to call ourselves *kalâtdlit* in front of your honorable head!

   3.) And making use of all that belonged to you, we feel a desire to advance; bettering the conditions, which hold you back, we are firmly resolved to go forward, forward.

References

Albertsen, Leif Ludwig 1978: *Lyrik der synges*. Berlingske Leksikon Bibliotek. Copenhagen. Berlingske Forlag.

Balle, Poul 1943: "National Festdag". *Grønlandsposten* 2(5):52.

Bartholdy, Nils G. 1986: "Grønlands flag". *Heraldisk Tidsskrift* 6 (53).

Berthelsen, Chr. 1983: *Grønlandsk litteratur: En kommenteret antologi*. Editor and translator, Chr. Berthelsen and Per Langgård. Aarhus. Centrum Publishers.

Bjerg, Hans Chr. 1974: "Grønlands våben og Den kongelige grønlandske Handels segl – Kalâtdlit-nunâta ilisarnaqutâ naqitsisâlo". *kgh orientering* May 16, 1974. Anniversary number. pp. 130-147.

Bjerg, Hans Chr. 1975: "Grønlands våben". *Heraldisk Tidsskrift* no. 31:39-48.

Christiansen, Hans C. 1962: "Mens tæppet går ned for det grønlandske pengevæsen". *Tidsskriftet Grønland* 10 (12):441-456.

Dahl, Jens 1986: *Arktisk selvstyre: historien bag og rammerne for det grønlandske hjemmestyre*. Copenhagen. Akademisk Forlag.

erinarsûtit 1913. (pingajugssânik naqitigkat) Nûk: ilíniarfigssûp naqiterivigtâne naqitigkat.

erinarsûtit 1967. (7-gssânik naqitigkat) (Photographic reprint of the sixth edition). Copenhagen.

Erinarsuutit 1980: Aqqissuisut: Karl J. Nielsen and John Egede. Nuuk: Kalaallit Nunaanni Naqiterisitsisarfik.

Feilberg, Jon, Bent Fredskild and Sune Holt 1984: *Grønlands Blomster – Flowers of Greenland*. Ringsted: Regnbuen Publishers.

Flensborg, Peter 1970: *Grønlandske pengesedler 1803-1967*. Copenhagen: Flensborg.

Foersom, Th., Finn O. Kapel and Ole Svarre 1982: *Nunatta naasui – Grønlands flora i farver*. Kalaallisut suliarinera Isak Heilmann. (1.ed. 1971) Nuuk: Pilersuiffik.

Foighel, Isi 1980: *Home Rule in Greenland. Meddelelser om Grønland. Man and Society* 1.

Folkehøjskolens sangbog 1989: Foreningen for folkehøjskoler i Danmark (ed.) 17th edition. Odense. Foreningens Forlag.

Frederiksen, Svend 1952: "Henrik Lund: a National Poet of Greenland". *Proceedings of the American Philosophical Society*, 96 (6):653-659.

Grønland: Danmark i Nord 1947. Copenhagen. Berlingske Tidende.

Grønlands Lommekalender 1988 1987. Grønlands Hjemmestyre (ed.). Nuuk.

Grønlands Landsråds forhandlinger 1948-1978. Nuuk.

Grønlands Landstings forhandlinger 1979-1983. Nuuk.

Haxthausen, Otto 1973: "Dronning Margrethe II's våben". *Heraldisk Tidsskrift* 3 (27):297-305.

Heilmann, Steffan 1985: "Skrivelse af 28.5.85 vedr. Grønlands nationaldag". *Ilulissat kommunalbestyrelses møde 11. juni 1985*: 7/85. case no. 1084 – journal no. 00.06.01. Ilulissat.

Hjald Carlsen, Per (ed.) 1960: *Med kongefamilien til Grønland – A Royal Visit*. Photographs by Allan Moe. Text by Bent Nielsen. Copenhagen: Illustrationsforlaget.

Hjort Christiansen, Benthe 1989: "Mosaik". *Niviarsiaq* 3 (12):7-1.

Hobsbawm, Eric and Terence Ranger (ed.) 1986: *The Invention of Tradition*. Past and Present Publications. Cambridge University Press.

Holm, Johan Chr 1957: "Grønlandske mønter". *Tidsskriftet Grønland* 5 (6):201-209.

Jensen, Peter 1979: *Thulep uumasui pingaarnerit*. Copenhagen: Ministery of Greenland.

Johansen, Lars Emil 1976: In: *Grønlands fremtid. Uddrag af en debat på kursus/konferenceejendommen Rolighed i Skodsborg*. Skodsborg: Rolighed. pp. 61-65.

Kalaallit Allakkeriviat/Grønlands Postvæsen og Det Grønlandske Selskab (eds.) 1988: *Grønland set gennem 50 års frimærker 1938-1988*. Rolf Gilberg, Gunnar Kaspersen, Mads Lidegaard and Eric V. Wowern (eds.). Copenhagen.

Kjær Sørensen, Axel 1979: "Grønlandsk nationalisme". *Historie, Jyske Samlinger, Ny Række* XIII (1-2):208-225.

Kleist, Josva 1922. "nánúniarneq". In: Karl Chemnitz (ed.): *piniarnermik ilitsersûtit*. Nûk: sineríssap kajatdliup naqiteriviane naqitigkat. pp. 34-37.

Kleist, Josva 1971: "Bjørnejagt". In: Keld Hansen (ed.): *Grønlandske fangere fortæller*. Foreword by Jørgen Meldgaard. Nordiske landes Publishers. pp. 63-66.

Kleivan, Helge 1969/70: "Culture and Ethnic Identity. On Modernization and Ethnicity in Greenland". *Folk* 11-12:209-234.

Kleivan, Inge 1969/70. "Language and Ethnic Identity: Language Policy and Debate in Greenland". *Folk* 11-12:235-285.

Kleivan, Inge 1985. "Debat og sprogbrug i forbindelse med dobbelte stednavne i Grønland". In: *Stednavne i brug. Festskrift udgivet i anledning af stednavneudvalgets 75 års jubilæum*. Bent Jørgensen (ed.). Copenhagen. C.A. Reitzels Forlag. pp. 140-161.

Kleivan, Inge 1988. "The creation of Greenland's new national symbol: the flag". *Folk* 30:33-56.

Kr. L. (= Kristoffer Lynge) 1933. "nunarput". *Atuagagdliutit* 73 (1): 4-5.

Langgård, Karen 1987: *Henrik Lunds verdslige digtning I-II*. Thesis, Institut for Eskimology. 1984. Nuuk: Ilisimatusarfik.

Larsen, Thor 1978: *The World of the Polar Bear*. With a Foreword by Sir Peter Scott. London. New York. Sidney. Toronto: Hamlyn.

Lauritzen, Philip 1982. *Dronningen i Grønland. 1000 år efter Erik den Røde*. Copenhagen. Rhodos.

Lynge, Bent 1943: "Om vor nationale Festdag". *Grønlandsposten* 2(5):53.

Lynge, Finn 1989: "How Danish are the Greenlanders, really?" Ilumut kalaallit qanoq danskiutigaat? In: Jens Dahl ed.: *Keynote Speeches from the Sixth Inuit Studies Conference, Copenhagen, October 1988. Institut for Eskimologi 14*. Copenhagen. University of Copenhagen. pp. 68-73; 7-14.

Nielsen, Frederik 1952: "uvdloq nagdliútorsiotarfigssaq? – En grønlandsk nationaldag?" *Atuagagdliutit/Grønlandsposten* 92 (23):396-398.

Nielsen, Frederik 1954: "kúngíkorsiorneq. aussame 1952-me kúngip Frederik IX-ata nuliatalo dronning Ingridip kalâtdlit nunânut tikerârnerat". Nuuk: kalâtdline qáumarsautigssîniaqatigît naqitertitât.

Nielsen, Frederik 1956: "Henrik Lund". In: *kalâtdlit taigdliortue tatdlimat – Fem grønlandske digtere*. Nuuk: Grønlands Kulturelle råd – Kalâtdlit-nunâne kulturåde. pp. 11-46.

Nielsen, Peter 1943: "Vore nationale Festdage". *Grønlandsposten* 2(2):15-16.

Petersen, Robert 1976: "Grønlænderne som et folk". *Information* November 2. Reprinted and translated into Greenlandic: "Kalâtdlit inuiagtut – Grønlænderne som et folk". *Atuagagdliutit/Grønlandsposten* 116(48):12-13.

Petersen, Robert 1985: "The Use of Certain Symbols in Connection with Greenlandic Identity". In: Jens Brøsted et.al. ed.: *Native Power: The Quest for Autonomy and Nationhood of Indigenous Peoples*. Bergen. Universitetsforlaget. pp. 294-300.

Rasmussen, Hans-Erik 1983: "Socio-symboler og etnopolitiske symboler i Grønland. Eksempler fra 1930-40'erne samt fra perioden ca. 1976-1982". In: *10. nordiske etnografmøde. København 20-22 oktober 1982: Hvad kan vi lære af andre kulturer: Antopologiens praktiske, teoretiske og kulturelle anvendelse i Norden i dag og i morgen*. Institute for Ethnology and Anthropology, University of Copenhagen. pp. 261-289.

Red. (= Christian Vibe) 1942: "Hvilke dage er Grønlands nationale festdage – og hvorledes kan og bør vi fejre dem?" *Grønlandsposten* 1(10):117.

Red (= Christian Vibe) 1943: "Vore Nationale Festdage". *Grønlandsposten* 2(5):53.

Saladin d'Anglure, Bernard 1990. "Nanook, super-male: the polar bear in the imaginary space and social time of the Inuit of The Canadian Arctic". In: R.G. Willis (ed): *Signifying Animals. One World Archaeology* 16: 178-195.

sic. (= Helge Christensen) 1959: "Den grønlandske isbjørn har rejst sig og fægter med de våde forlabber – Kalâtdlit-nunâta nanua nikússârpoq isigkaminigdlo masagtunik anaussigalugtuardlune". Atuagagdliutit/Grønlandsposten 99(2):8-9.

Siumut partiip nipaa 1979. 5(90).

Thalbitzer, William 1916: "Grønlandske Sommerdage ved Kap Farvel". *Atlanten* XIII(149):309-332.

Thalbitzer, William 1926: *Arktiske digte og hjemlige. Fra Grønland til Helsingør*. Copenhagen. H. Ascheoug & Co.

Thalbitzer, William 1939: *Inuit Sange og Danse fra Grønland – Inuit Songs and Dances from Greenland – Inuit kalâliussut erinarssûtaisa qitataisalo ilait*. Copenhagen. Munksgaard.

Thalbitzer, William 1945: *Grønlandske digte og danske. Gamle og nye kvad*. Copenhagen. Ejnar Munksgaards Publishers.

Thuesen, Søren 1988: *Fremad, opad. Kampen for en moderne grønlandsk identitet*. Copenhagen. Rhodos.

Vibe, Christian 1981: "Isbjørn, Ursus maritimus, Nanoq". In: Finn Salomonsen (ed): *Grønlands Fauna: Fisk, Fugle, Pattedyr*. Copenhagen. Gyldendal. pp. 383-387.

Vibe, Christian 1985: "Nanoq, Ursus maritimus, Isbjørn". In: Finn Salomonsen (ed): *Kalaallit Nunaata Uumasui*. Nuuk: Kalaallit Nunaanni Naqiteritsisarfik. pp. 383-387.

Universitetets Mindefest i to Hundredaaret for Hans Egedes Ankomst til Grønland, 1921. University of Copenhagen.

The Role of Research in the Construction of Greenlandic Identity

Robert Petersen

ABSTRACT

The question of Greenlandic identity is addressed in historical perspective. Focus is upon the dynamic relationship between "Greenlandic" and "Danish", as it unfolds in the course of changing structural and cultural relations between the two countries. At issue is the multiple identities resulting from the co-existence of Greenlanders and Danes a structure separating the two groups and yet creating conditions where Danes within form part of Greenlandic society and public opinion.

Introduction

We may assume that identity in prehistoric Greenland was connected to the specificity of the culture just as it is today – to the extent, that is, that members of the different cultures had a chance to meet at all. There can be no doubt that Inuit and Tornit, for example, belonged to two different social groups, and I believe the legends to be based on real-life events, since they distinguish between Tornit and Inuit and refer to Tornit as alien. All the same, however, the development of the Eastern Greenlandic dialect during prehistoric time suggests a rather close communication between members of the two groups. Some sort of cultural intermixture seems to precondition this development, which may, eventually, be subjected to archaeological research.

Within the boundaries of the individual ethnic-cultural group, however, the criteria of group identity seem to have been defined by the regional distribution of people.

Identity formation in colonial and post-colonial time

Greenlanders' perception of self was under development for a long time without any outside interference. In the beginning Greenlanders made a rather homogeneous ethnic group. In historical time, however, when the Scandinavians arrived and ethnically mixed marriages were formed, a line was drawn between Greenlanders and Danes. Criteria of distinction were based on descent and occupation. The language carried no power of distinction, since all children spoke Greenlandic. The categorization developed as follows:

1) Persons of mixed parentage, involved in Greenlandic occupations or married to persons occupied in Greenlandic trades, were considered Greenlanders.

2) Persons of mixed parentage, who picked an artisanal or a literary occupation as their first choice, were counted as Danes.

3) Gradually, however, as individuals considered Greenlandic entered into artisanal jobs, it came to be that those in superior positions were the ones to be defined as Danes.

Already in the early period of colonial history this scheme was further elaborated by the fact that members of households headed by Greenlandic men frequently became hunters and fishermen, as did the members of households headed by Greenlandic men in lower positions. The crudity of the underlying cultural criterium soon made the above 1-3 distinction non-operational in terms of social functioning and gave way to the language criterium.

The function of language as a criterion of ethnic identity, however, was even now connected to parental heritage. Children of Danish couples coming from Denmark and occupying superior positions would never be counted as Greenlanders, even if their primary language was Greenlandic. But children of Greenlandic and mixed marriages, who spoke primarily Greenlandic, were considered Greenlanders.

Until after 1950 the use of Greenlandic was a defining characteristic of the language use in any household. Children of mixed couples were always considered Greenlanders and often chose "Greenlandic" occupations such as hunting and fishing or inferior positions in the state administration. Their social networks were primarily Greenlandic.

Societal developments and cultural changes caused even this criterion to lose its power of distinction. As we approach the period after 1950 a situation developed, in which children in Greenlandic towns in many cases actually never learned to speak Greenlandic. We are not only talking about Danish and mixed marriages. Children from socalled "pure" Greenlandic families were also found in this situation, which stimulated the construction of new categories of identification. The Greenlandic language may from this time on be considered a language of powerlessness or impotence, since it could never be used for career purposes. As in many other colonized countries, parents encouraged their children to learn the language of the colonizers (Skutnabb-Kangas 1987: 57). Danish speaking children of mixed marriages could become Danes. This situation, however, was often biased, since Greenlanders considered them to be Danes, whereas Danes considered them to be Greenlanders. Since they were never considered integral members of the group in which they found themselves, these individuals developed problems of identity (Petersen 1985: 300).

The Danish speaking children of parents with a Greenlandic identity are more difficult to place. They never actually placed themselves – we may say that they have no self-evident identity. Although they may feel their Greenlandic identity strengthened in some way, they are placed in the Danish group with which they associate. This category of individuals appears to have difficulties getting acceptance by others as well as obtaining full membership of a particular group.

Yet another category of identity should be mentioned – the one experienced by individuals who arrived on a work-contract, remained in Greenland when the contract expired and maybe married and raised a family. They often consider themselves to be "Greenlanders", even if they are unable to speak Greenlandic. We do not know as yet how big this group is, nor how others respond to the members' definition of their own self. I take it that this personal identification with Greenland derives from actual partaking in Greenlandic society. It may be that the use of the term "Greenlander" does not refer to perception of identity in a bi-ethnic community but is, rather, used to state one's citizenship of the Greenlandic society.

The identity debate in early 20th Century Greenland

In the years between 1910 and 1920 a debate arose about what it takes to be a Greenlander. The debate was carried on from two positions. The one party maintained that a genuine Greenlander possessed a qajaq and lived by hunting and fishing (Thorning 1917). The other argued that whoever spoke Greenlandic was a Greenlander, no matter the occupation (Lynge 1913; Petersen 1918; Lynge 1919). The import-

ance of descent was never included in the debate, although it lingers in the background.

For a while this latter definition was accepted as valid – for those living in Greenland, whose parents were Greenlandic and who spoke the national language. As a Greenlander living in Denmark, however, one was considered Greenlandic on basis of descent alone, the Greenlandic language had no importance (Petersen 1985: 300).

During this period of identity debate it was never questioned, whether a person was submitted to Danish or Greenlandic law, nor if a person was born in or outside of Greenland. These questions were never raised explicitly in the identity debate, although they seemed to be recognized when the debate referred to figures like "44.000 Greenlanders" or even "Greenlandic-speakers". Whereas *public statistics* simply intended to refer to "persons born in Greenland", the *identity debate* was concerned with whether or not an individual had Greenlandic ancestors and was able to speak Greenlandic (Kleivan 1969: 78).

Even if the debate primarily circled around these questions, the sense of identity seemed to relate to other aspects as well. Somehow it seems to have mattered, for instance, if a person "ate Greenlandic". It is not quite clear how and why, and the indication was mostly heard in connections like: "Why can't you, a Greenlander, eat this food?" which seems to indicate that being a Greenlander one was expected to like certain foods. The notion was especially raised in connection with dishes prepared on traditional foodstuffs by way of boiling, drying or smoking, or simply with raw foods. Such foods are often eaten in the company of many people and often on festive occasions. Maybe it was these social aspects of the eating traditions that invoked the sense of identity – more than the food itself. In other words, I do not think that the notion of "eating Greenlandic" has anything to do with the phrase that "people are what they eat".

Another dimension entered into day-to-day interaction connected to the idea of "Greenlandic" and "Danish" trades or occupations. Criteria for this distinction were of two kinds. One referring to a notion of "natural" or "household" economy, one referring to "efficiency". According to these criteria people were sometimes identified according to occupation, which lead to the development of a vaguely formulated notion allocating individuals to categories of people characterised as "thinking Greenlandic" and "thinking Danish", respectively. Somehow this categorisation implies the idea that "humaneness" is opposed to "efficiency" – a humane attitude in this case meaning that a person is foremost humane and first then efficient. The postulated idea that some found it more important to be efficient than humane was for some reason identified as "Danish thinking".

If we take the attitudes of "humanity" and "efficiency" to be the fundamental characteristics of Greenlanders versus Danes, or if it is generally taken to be the granted truth by Greenlanders and Danes alike, we are running into a very dangerous situation: It is somehow assumed that there are tasks, which should not be commissioned to Greenlanders, since they are unable to accomplish them. Consequently, the Danes will have to do these jobs.

It seems reasonable to assume that this "discourse of inefficiency" which somehow came to imbue the way of thinking during this time can be traced to Danish civil servants, whose presence and role was thereby legitimated. However, the notion was taken over by the Greenlanders themselves, as we have seen it happen in other colonized territories. Considering that a feeling of incompetence may prejudice the active participation of individuals in social affairs, we may wonder about the detrimental implications for a whole community.

In traditional society not all individuals possessed the same degree or kinds of competence either. The more outstanding or "efficient" individuals were leaders and great hunters. The less competent made more "ordinary" contributions to society. The danger inherent in the picture forming in Greenland during this period was that people came to identify with the less outstanding individuals – not with the great hunters.

This way of thinking must of course be seen in connection with the idea that the Danes came as "civilizers", who brought "culture" and "progress" and solved all problems above household level. This led to a feeling of gratitude, which, strange as it may seem, was most apparent among the better educated in Greenland. It also furthered the creation of a silent majority, which may be the reason that the period is often talked about by Danish civil servants as a period of "harmony".

An article in the Greenlandic newspaper *Avannaamioq* in 1917 took the view that citizens of the same state shared common norms, but the author did not elaborate the question further ("Qeqertarsuup tunuamioq" 1917).

Another dimension of identity was a certain aloofness from traditional society. The traditional Greenlanders did not read and write. They were not Christians. They were "Eskimos" (Sandgreen 1982). The reason that identity came to be mixed up with the Christian church may well be related to the fact that influence of alternative religious faiths did not occur due to Greenland's isolation as a Danish colony. Consequently, all Greenlanders belonged to one and the same church, and Greenlandic became church language at a very early stage (Kleivan 1979: 132).

A curious duality is sensed in this period in way of reference. An individual may well in one situation refer to a Danish ancestor and in another talk about "our ancestors", meaning Inuit in the old days. – The same observation has been related to me by researchers doing kinship studies in Greenland, even if the Danish/ Norwegian element soon came to dominate the genealogies because of the way kinship was recorded in colonial time. Dualities of this kind may be explained, I believe, by the fact that people think of their heritage in terms of different affinities. On the one hand they refer to their genealogical relations, on the other hand to their relationships of cultural identity. – As I understand it, reference to the Inuit forefathers was not only connected to a notion of genealogy, but also to a notion of ethnic and cultural heritage shared with other Inuit. At the same time, Greenlanders did not want to repudiate the European part of their cultural and genealogical heritage.

The point is that throughout this period we can discern a certain sense of respect and admiration of these Inuit ancestors, who "managed" without outside help, coupled with an attitude of distance towards traditional society, as mentioned above. Something in this ambivalence towards own culture suggests that Greenlanders from the first half of this century saw themselves as not measuring up to their ancestors – nor to the Greenlanders of future generations who could be expected to be able to manage on their own.

Before leaving the early 20th century debate on identity, I want to call attention to Hans A. Lynge, the Greenlandic author who, in 1988, wrote an article on this matter. The occasion was a radio programme, in which it was claimed that the vernacular was the decisive criterion of identity. Lynge disagreed with this point, analysed the debate carried on 1910-1920 in *"Kalaallit oqaluttuarisaanerat"*, and described the change in identity symbolism which occurred during these years. He went on to suggest that other symbols of identity might be found than the ones, he himself had come across, and that a thorough discussion be taken so as to examine their importance (Lynge and Larsen 1987: 126).

The role of research in the construction of identity

The prevailing sense of Greenlandic identity in this period seems to contain several levels or dimensions. From one perspective, identity construction seemed to build on the contrast between people you knew and people you did not know. From this point of view even Greenlanders in remote places were foreigners. But if we look at identity in terms of relations between Greenlanders and Danes in Greenland, descendents of Greenlandic parents and individuals who spoke Greenlandic as their first language were Greenlanders in opposition to the Danes (who were not). I know of only one group of brothers and sisters, who by local people were considered to be Greenlanders, although both parents were Danish (Petersen 1985: 297).

Hans-Erik Rasmussen has made an interesting analysis of the development of the symbolic content of Greenlandic women's clothing. Rasmussen comments on a series of photos of Karoline Rosing depicted in situations where she is wearing different kinds of clothes. Apparently, and I agree with the conclusions drawn by Rasmussen, she dressed differently in consideration of the context of appearance. When she wears Greenlandic clothes, Rasmussen points out that she wishes to define herself as a Greenlandic woman. Two instances, in which she wears a European dress, are interpreted as marking different terms of identity. – On the one occasion, it is suggested, Karoline Rosing defines herself as a Greenlandic civil servant, whereas on the other she identifies herself with the Danes. It should be added here that she was married to a Dane and was one of the few Greenlanders at the time, who spoke Danish. I believe that Rasmussen is right in all three cases (Rasmussen, pers. comm.).

From the late 1960s, research came to play a certain role in the formation of Greenlandic identity. – Not a spectacular role, i.e. directly influencing the terms of identity construction. Nonetheless, it contributed to an understanding of the processes at play in the development of a more heterogeneous society and of the structural conditions shaping the context in which Greenland found herself. This sense of structure gave theoretical support for the political arguments in favour of a more independent Greenland. An ethnic awakening was witnessed these years, as was an increasingly heterogeneous society. Eskimologists and anthropologists sided very much with the Greenlanders against the institutions and decisions which gradually encroached upon their control of land and their way of life. Studies on Greenlanders as an ethnic group and a 4th world people were available to the public to an extent that makes it quite plausible that research did, in fact, influence the terms, in which the experience of being a Greenlander was and is discussed.

The categorisation of Greenlanders as a 4th world people, as far as I can see, resulted from the work of anthropologists and eskimologists on the one hand, and Greenlanders in Denmark on the other hand. It was the early 1970s, in particular the period around the Arctic Peoples' Conference in 1973 in Copenhagen and, subsequently, the formation of the World Council of Indigeneous Peoples in 1975. For Greenlanders, these were occasions for a wholly new and global approach to an understanding of their own situation. With reference to Greenlanders' perception of themselves, new terms developed such as "minority", which applies to something very different from a "population". Newspapers these years often asked the question, whether the inhabitants of Bornholm (a

Danish island in the Baltic Sea) did not also deserve minority status? The newspapers, it appeared, put more weight on numbers than they did on culture and ethnicity. This press commentary, however joking, became a dimension of a certain consequence in the Greenlandic political debate, where questions of minority rights and minority protection were topics of the day (Olsen 1978: 60). The notion of minority and the public Danish response to demands formulated in terms of claims to minority status, was an important factor in the construction of a Greenlandic identity. In fact, I think it played a central part in the development of the home rule concept since it legitimised arguments in favour of it. Before the minority dimension entered the debate, "home rule" was a political taboo word. Jørgen Olsen, a well known member of the Greenlandic National Council *(Landsråd),* who was the first to raise the issue in the 1960s was in the *Landsråd* asked to make a public apology for the mere suggestion of home rule (Fleischer 1989: 4).

Identity can therefore be dealt with on a scale progressively expressing or encompassing ethnic group, national minority and, finally – with the introduction of Home Rule – we can talk about a nation encompassing two ethnic groups (Sara 1986: 12).

There is another perspective on the question of how research can be said to have influenced the construction of Greenlandic identity. By their advocacy of 'the way of the Greenlanders', it can be said that eskimologists have promoted the idea of a "Greenlandic way of thinking" implying "humanity" rather than "efficiency". The values stressed here are good and beautiful! However, the idea of a particular Greenlandic way of thinking constructs an image of "the Greenlander" as being someone, who let things go by, who is limited in what s(he) can do (sometimes someone, who should rather not be able to do certain things, or else s(he) is not a real Greenlander). We need just remind ourselves that this characterisation of Greenlanders leaves no room for the outstanding individuals in traditional society to see that such a depiction of real Greenlandic identity has dangerous implications.

In relation to modern realities of Greenlandic society this stereotypical image of the Greenlander does not hold. It is, in fact, an open question, if we can continue seing Greenlanders as a homogeneous group. What was described for the early 20th century was a situation in which Danish/Greenlandic identity was related to occupation. Today, however, other terms of identity have developed which relate to membership of social groups based on criteria cutting across ethnicity. We are perhaps led to modify our notion of cultural identity, since the perception of identity differs among members of an ethnic group depending on their belonging to different categories within the overall "group". Each category maintains a specific combination of ethnically relevant factors or symbols of identity. Individual members do not necessarily subscribe to each and every criteria (see also Paine, this vol.). In fact, the individual combination of criteria of content and/or structure constituting identity varies at different intersections between relationships to category and group. When setting out to define Greenlandic identity, we have to consider the time and context we are dealing with. A rough periodisation has already been suggested above, albeit implicitly. Let me repeat: We may assume that groups and subgroups in late prehistoric time were distinguished in terms of region, whereas from early historic time subdifferentiation came to be in terms of cultural criteria. Nowadays the situation is more complex. Subgroups defined by cultural criteria (Greenlanders as opposed to Danes) as well as subgroups defined by structural criteria (Greenlanders as opposed to other Inuit) are crosscut by subgroups based on interest (associations). I very much doubt, where a possible opposition between urban and village Greenlanders should be located in this structure. An opposition of this kind, however, *is* part of the complex picture that is developing in Greenland.

An aspect of being a Greenlander is connected to the fact of Greenland possessing its own political party system separate from the Danish party system. In addition to the cultural and ethnic dimension, the Atlantic Ocean separating Denmark and Greenland has made it easier to conceive of the two countries as distinct entities attached through their common constitution. This *"rigsfællesskab"* (unity of the realm) between the two countries is mentioned in the political programmes of both *Siumut* and *Atassut,* the largest political parties in Greenland. Both parties take it as a precondition, but whereas Atassut takes its point of departure in this fact, Siumut only mentions it after the presentation of the "Greenlandic conditions". It is fair to say that Atassut from its start has always supported the idea of a Greenlandic *structural identity,* i. e. an identity qua part of the union. Siumut, on the other hand, from the start stressed the *cultural dimension* of Greenlandic identity. A result of this difference has been that Danes with little knowledge of Greenlandic politics have demonstrated a marked sympathy for Atassut. In this connection it has been claimed that the strong position of Atassut in Nuuk owes itself to the fact that there are many Danish voters living in Nuuk. We do not know, whether this has ever been true. Results of the latest municipal election seem to indicate that it is not as simple as that. Danes in Greenland voted for different political parties.

The establishment of *Ilisimatusarfik*, Greenland's university, in 1983 was important for several reasons. Being an educational and research institution in its own right, Ilisimatusarfik is part of and an expression of a modern Greenlandic identity. A primary purpose of the university is to engage in research in identity related questions that rise out of the very context in which it is situated. This may contribute to the creation of a more dynamic conception of what constitutes Greenlandic identity.

It is difficult to separate the contribution of Ilisimatusarfik and anthropological research in general to the construction of identity from that of the general debate. However, certain points have been made by researchers, which have subsequently entered into the discussion. – Archaeologist have brought evidence of the prehistoric connection between Greenland, Canada and Alaska, which is an important part of cultural identity in present day Greenland. Anthropological influence has centred on the use of the concept of minority and Greenland's relationship to the 4th world, which has no doubt influenced the way Greenlanders conceive of the world and their place in it. – The contribution from research is not all to the establishment of a content or a context of identity. Research has also been critical in the sense that it has commented on the potential intolerant tendencies inherent in a too narrow focus on the content of identity or the content of "Greenlandicness". It may be argued that anthropologists have helped turn the perspective from heritage to the broader question of culture. When people today talk about their "Inuit kinsmen", what they are implying is an identification on the basis of culture.

This cultural distinction coexists with a structural distinction in the cases where Greenlanders distinguish themselves from other Inuit and when Danes in Greenland shake their heads over Copenhagen etc. The perception of structural distance is like provincialism in Denmark, in the sense that it expresses peripheral discontent with central authorities. However, this structural distinction from Denmark felt in Greenland contains other dimensions as well, since it is often expressed by sympathetic Danes siding with Greenlandic society. Since the very same Danes may well be opposed to the expression "Inuit kinsmen", I think we can conclude that certain Danes feel themselves to be part of Greenlandic society and possess a Greenlandic identity, yet do not identify themselves with the Inuit.

In day-to-day life, I believe that considerations of descent from Greenlandic ancestors, who may well be of mixed descent, and the ability to speak Greenlandic are still factors of great importance to the formation of Greenlandic identity. There is no doubt, however, that individuals have gained acceptance as Greenlanders, even if they are found at the other side of the line created by these criteria. Since it is becoming more usual that individuals, who do not speak Greenlandic and who cannot even point to Greenlandic ancestors, define themselves as Greenlanders, I think we can expect this boundary to be moved again – maybe in the direction of a more unitary and hence stronger sense of common Greenlandic identity.

Concluding remarks

One of the factors contributing to the varied picture presented as the Greenlandic identity or rather, *Greenlandic identities*, is the coexistence of Greenlanders and Danes within a structure separating the two groups and yet, especially in modern time, creating conditions where the Danes form part of the public opinion in Greenland in opposition to the official Danish position. This structural separation is supported by the fact that Danes who are residents of Greenland form part of the Greenlandic political system and can vote only for political candidates in Greenland.

Another part in the formation of identity is played by the day-to-day contexts of social interaction, in which individuals may find themselves in situations ambiguously drawing on one or the other criterion of identification thus promoting the formation of similarly ambiguous identities.

It should be pointed out, concludingly, that the common Greenlandic-Danish identity, i.e. the structural identity, thrives when Denmark participates in international sports competitions – especially when they are directly transmitted on TV. What happens afterwards, we do not know yet.

References

Fleischer, Jørgen 1989. "Vejen mod Hjemmestyre. – Fødestedskriteriet og talen om masseafvandring." *Sermitsiaq no. 22, June 2.*

Kleivan, Inge 1969. "Sprogproblemet." In: Jan Hjarnø (ed.), *Grønland i fokus.* Nationalmuseet. København.

Lynge, B. 1919. "Eqqarsaatinnguaq kalaallisut inuuneq atassutisaalu pillugit". – ('Thoughts about the Greenlandic way of life and how it can be saved'). – *Avannaamioq.*

Lynge, Frederik 1913. "Kalaaliussuserput qanoq atsigisumik pigissavarput?" – ('How much should we hold on to our identity as Greenlanders?'). – *Avannaamioq.*

Lynge, Hans A. 1987. (Together with Magnus Larsen): "Anersaakkut timikkullu eqiilerneq." – ('Spiritual and cultural awakening'). In: H. C. Petersen, Hans Anthon Lynge et al (eds.), *Kalaallit oqaluttuarisaanerat I.* Nuuk.

Lynge, Hans A. 1988. "Asasara Kaj Peter Svendsen". – ('Dear Kaj Peter Svendsen'). *A/G Aliikutassiaq, Nov.30.*

Olsen, M. 1978. "Moses Olsens tale i Folketinget i 1971," – Mads Lidegaard (ed.), Politiske taler. *Tidsskriftet Grønland.*

Petersen, J. 1918. "Isummanut aporaattunut". – ('Comments on the (identity) debate'). *Avannaamioq.*

Petersen, Robert 1984. "Kalaaliussuseq". – ('Being a Greenlander'). Inaugural lecture at Ilisimatusarfik.

Petersen, Robert 1985. "The use of some symbols in connection with Greenlandic identity". In: Jens Brøsted et al (eds.), *Native Power.* Universitetsforlaget: Bergen, Oslo, Stavanger, Tromsø.

Qeqertarsuup tunuamioq 1917: "Upernavimmiumut akissut." – ('Answer to an Upernavimmioq'). – *Avannaamioq.*

Qupersiman, Georg 1982. *Min eskimoiske fortid.* Ed. by Otto Sandgreen. København.

Sara, A. S. 1986. *Samisk høyere utdanning og forskning.* Nordisk Samisk Institut: Kautokeino.

Skutnabb-Kangas, Tove 1986. *Minoritet, språk och rasism.* Malmø.

Thorning, Jakob 1917. "Kalaallit angallataannit suna pingaarnerua?" – ('What is the most important Greenlandic means of transportation'). – *Avannaamioq.*

Trails of Saami Self-Consciousness

Robert Paine

ABSTRACT

A cluster of issues are addressed: How Saami have handled a stigmatized identity vis-à-vis the Norwegian; how a rewarding sense of 'being Saami' has been expressed within local communities; how striving for a 'national' expression provokes ethno-political struggles among themselves and not just vis-à-vis the Norwegians. And – how do Saami intellectuals handle non-Saami writings about these issues?

Introduction

I wish to begin by considering three general issues, the first of which is *Wittgenstein's family resemblances.*

Let me remind you what is meant by that: A population may share a number of characteristics – A through to F, for instance. We may say – loosely or precisely – that this population constitutes a "culture". However (Wittgenstein insists), no one individual or even sub-group within the population will possess exactly the same combination of characteristics. Thus characteristic F will be missing in one case, E in another, D in yet another, and so forth. In general terms, this draws attention to (among other things) *patterned diversity* within a culture.

And why should this be of concern to us? It directs us to *how* Inuit (here I include Greenlanders within that family of resemblances) or *how* Saami recognize each other – supposing they do.

Given the wide diversity of situations in which Inuit, or Saami, interact these days – different occupations, levels of education, lifestyles, even different citizenship (Soviet, American, Canadian or Greenlandic; Norwegian, Swedish, Finnish or Soviet) – it seems to me important to recognize the centrality of this issue with its *two* levels of question: Do you/they recognize each other? If so, how?

Let us also keep in mind – as I suppose was the intention of the conference convenors when they included a presentation about the Saami in the midst of papers about Greenlandic culture! – that such "families" of resemblances may be serial. In one context the Inuit and the Saami are separate "families", but in the Fourth World and/or northern peoples context(s) they combine.

However, for my present purpose I place the emphasis differently: We should not allow ourselves unexamined assumptions about ethnic homogeneity and, even more serious perhaps, about ethnic solidarity.

To take an example from another part of the world: American Jews usually claim that they can recognize each other but the Jewishness of English Jews is likely to be hidden from them – all they see are English men & women. But Israelis, one can always recognize them, anywhere! My source is the best there is – my wife (Jewish, American-born, one-time Israeli). Nevertheless, most of us don't *test* this knowledge we suppose we have – and *there* is an important point.

With respect to the Saami, there appear to be 'soft' or porous and 'hard' sides to that boundary: The Finnish and Norwegian/Swedish sides, respectively. The Finnish and Saami languages share family resemblances from which Norwegian and Swedish are excluded. Occupationally, too, there are affinities (including participation in reindeer pastoralism) between northern Finns and Saami that are weaker or absent between Saami and Norwegians or Swedes.

At this point I should quickly convey some basic facts concerning the Saami.[1] Gross census figures (sociologically insensitive, they provide no more than some bench remarks as to absolute and relative sizes[2]) put the Saami population in Norway at 30.000, in Sweden at 15.000, in Finland at 5000, and on the Kola Peninsula in the Soviet Union at 2000.

In Norway – the domain for most of what I will have to say – 24.000 of that 30.000 live in the two northernmost provinces; that is, 15.000 in Finmark and 9000 in Troms. However, within the Saami population of these two provinces there are marked differences between those of the coast and of the interior (tundra). The formal markers of such differences are linguistic and occupational. In the interior, there are fewer than ten percent non-Saami speakers; this ratio is *reversed* along the coast on account of "Norwegianization", and is a matter of serious cultural consequence since the coast is where the majority of Saami have lived. Occupationally, seasonal transhumance lasted well into this century along the coast where fjordal fishing and small-scale farming, often in combination, remain the primary occupation today. The reindeer pastoralists – perhaps 2000 persons in the two provinces together – use coastal pastures in the summer but 'belong' to the tundra and such villages as Karasjok, Kautokeino, and Masi. It is there that they pay their local taxes. There is also a sedentary population living on the tundra, in those same villages and in small settlements strung along river courses, practicing a mixed subsistence and monetary economy of different combinations.

But behind these formal markers of difference – between coast and interior, sedentary and nomad – there are a host of behavioural differences. Indeed, these latter obtain even within the same community, if most usually between persons separated by generations and/or education. There arises – as we will see – serious ambiguities and even contradictions among Saami about being Saami, and about what one should do, if anything, about that.

Here it is as well to note that in Finmark the Saami (following the official statistics) account for somewhere between one fifth and one sixth of the provincial population; and in Troms perhaps no more than every sixteenth person "is" a Saami. Note, too, that in both provinces there is a third ethnicity (besides Norwegian and Saami) and that is Finnish, or *Kvaen*, peasant immigrants principally from the last century.

The second general issue is – as signalled in my title – that of *self-consciousness*.

How can I possibly suppose that I am competent to speak about self-consciousness of the Saami? And yet in a conference enquiring into nationalism and cultural identity, it is reasonable enough to want to consider self-consciousness. A lot has been written about the Saami, *but who does the writing?* May be that will tell us where we can find out about Saami self-consciousness.

There are some classical writings by Saami (in Saami originally) about their way of life and written in the first person; among these are Turi (1910), Baer (1926), Pirak (1933), and Skum (1955); also from this period, Larsen (1912) handled cultural identity in the genre of the novel. Larsen has been followed, two generations later, by Mankok and Sarri Nordrå, and in poetry, by Utsi (1970) and Valkeapaa (1974).[3] There are others besides.

But even through the 1960s, "Lappologi" really belonged to clerics and linguists – names such as J. A. Friis (of *Laila* fame), Jacob Fellman, Just Qvigstad, K. B. Wiklund, Konrad Nielsen, T. I. Itkonen, Björn Collinder, and Asbjörn Nesheim – none of whom were Saami. Zero Saami self-consciousness (and zero of their own).

Such was still very much the situation at the time of the first of the Nordic Saami Conferences in Jokkmokk in 1953,[4] though there were several prominent Saami figures by that time; two of whom – Israel Ruong and Hans Henriksen – had been brought into the fold of "Lappologues" by none less than Professors Collinder and Nielsen, respectively. Ruong (who eventually had a personal professorship at Uppsala in Finno-Ugric) had been Collinder's "amanuensis" for years – he would have been a great ethnographer![5] Henriksen (while earning his living in a mundane job in Oslo) was Nielsen's assistant in the compilation of the great Norwegian and English Lapp Dictionary. Henriksen ended up as the key representative from Norway on the Nordic Saami Council.

But times have changed a bit, or considerably, depending on how you measure it. There are *two* lists of writers, lists A and B: Non-Saami and Saami, respectively. Symbolically, at all events, list B is a little longer than list A. Certainly by the 60s, the Nordic Conferences were "Saami" (rather than "Lappologue") occasions.

Maybe, though, the lists are better portrayed as "teams" A & B which, at times, play "against" each other. And team B members are very likely to regard academics (that is to say, all of team A) as disqualified when it comes to talking/writing about Saami self-consciousness.

But to ensure that things aren't too neat and symmetrical – with clear either/or loyalties – a number of team B members are academics.

Furthermore, *there is a C team* – non-Saami by parentage (in a few cases, mixed Nwg.-Saami) but raised in a Saami world as much as in a Norwegian one. Many of them are academics.

So who does qualify to tell us about Saami self-consciousness?

It is *not* sufficient to say team B: Some have tackled the issue, others of them seem to studiously avoid it. And team A (mine), likewise. The difference is, of course, that when team B people speak/write about Saami self-consciousness it is based on their *own* experience (which is not without problematic implications, as we will see) and when team A members do, it is based on *others'* experiences. Possibly team C – as a kind of *metis*! – would be the most interesting. In all cases (and not just those of team A) there will be problems of interpretation and of generalization.

So what do I conclude from this?

1. there is no one entity – "Saami self-consciousness", but many trails to follow;
2. that I cannot assume competence, nevertheless I undertake to follow some "trails" – beware, then, my interpretive and generalizing pretensions!

I have decided to look (for the most part) at what *one person* has had to say – or write. Somebody from team A who has been around for a good while. I choose myself! (Of course there will be 'digressions' to others.) After all, this cuts out another level of interpretation. It should also mean that I'll be able to explain –

should you ask or should you wish to challenge me – the *context* of my remarks.

The last of the three general issues is what I call the *temptation of chronology*. My point here is that it is all too easy to accept what I am going to tell you as a *narrative* and to see the changes that fill the narrative as *progress*.

To an extent this is "true" – i.e. people sometimes see it this way themselves. After all our story *begins*, in the 50s, with a fractured minority people, the majority of whom carry a stigmatized identity, and *ends* on October 9th this year with the convening of a Saami parliament in the presence of a Norwegian king.

But it is an illusion in serious respects. Underneath the surface of glittering political triumph, we must ask what cognitive changes have taken place within the "family of resemblances" called Saami? What changes in everyday behaviour and attitudes? And far from the everyday, what changes in reaction to crisis? For that matter, how correct is it to speak of political triumph?

Now a brief word on my *organizational framework*.

Bearing in mind what I have said about the dispersion of the Saami, – geographically, ecologically, and culturally (incl. linguistically) – I distinguish between *social levels* of self-consciousness:

"community"   vs.   "nation" or supra-community
= unitary   = pluralist
(with respect to values, sanctions, rewards etc.)

So it is not self-consciousness itself that I look at but, rather, trails of behaviour which, I suggest, emerge, 'socialized', from it – that's all I can reach; the dynamics of an *individual's* consciousness of him- or herself elude me.[6]

For "community" I focus on the Laestadian congregation – a fundamentalist movement from early in the nineteenth century which saturated Saami- and Finnish-speaking communities in northern FennoScandia. When I was in the field through the 50s and 60s there was scarcely a Saami village without such a congregation. Furthermore: The congregation was just about synonymous with the adult, or at least married, community; and emphasis was placed on collective self-consciousness.

At the level of "nation" or supra-community, I look at the principal Saami national associations in Norway.

However, the question is, how does one proceed from the lower to the higher level? How do the few activate the many to this end? I answer this (answer by illustration) in two sections labelled "Ludic Bridges". I invoke the notion of *play* to communicate the temper of the times – experimental and idealistic, fearful and cynical, and above all else, self-reflexive. By *bridge*, of course, I wish to invoke passage, movement – but let it be noted that this 'traffic' does not always flow in the one progressive, emancipatory direction.

There are two of these 'bridging' sections because the affairs of the pastoralists and their sense of self cannot be subsumed under those of the non-pastoral Saami. Community-as-congregation, for example, does not help us towards the reindeer pastoralists' sense of self. They have never doubted who they are, culturally; never doubted their self-worth. "Norwegianization" has been held at bay. But their cultural prerogatives have often been under external pressure and blatantly attacked at times. Double ironies are embedded here: Governments rue their lack of control over the pastoralists even as they present them as embodying the "true" (Nwg. *ekte*) Saami culture, and that raises the ire of other Saami. One consequence is the marked strain of symbolic opposition in relations with the Norwegian officialdom and, as well, other Saami.

We are now ready to begin.

Community – congregation

Sitting, listening, for countless hours, in Laestadian meetings, I sensed a distinction at play between *doing* and *being*. The church *does*, the preachers were forever telling us. That is, it created God in its own likeness. But we believe, the preachers assured their congregations, God created man in His own likeness and so it is left to us *to be* – not to reach for salvation by such 'doings' (*gjerninger*) as the use of prayer & the sacraments.

Elsewhere I have written (Paine 1988a):

> *"The essence of the distinction between 'being' and 'doing' is time. To do is predicated on the passage of time but to be is to hold time still. To do, is to set a cause in motion that will be rewarded, in time, by its effects; but to be carries its own reward – it is both cause and effect. The Laestidians would like to be, timelessly, God's Children" (p.36).*

Further:

> *"/ It seemed as though/ in the space of each meeting Laestadians re-enact their spiritual history. Timeless and without linearity in the ordinary way, biblical events, events pertaining to Luther and to Laestadius, and contemporary relations with Norwegians, are blended together. ..."*

> *"Experientally, / each meeting/ is about the transformation of a congregation of sinners to a congregation of reborn. But also week after week, year after year through a century and a half, the 'death' and 'rebirth' of the hundreds of village congregations has also been a major force keeping alive a sense of being Saami, as opposed to the stigmatized 'Lapp'" (p.37).*

I believe the achievement of redemptive, collective self-consciousness is achieved in and by the congregation in three phases (Fig.1).

Phase 1: The preachers' message is that the access of the Saami ("you") to God has been severely controlled by the clergy ("them"); this is a subversion of the religious relationship. The clergy are "Nicodemuses" or "thieves of the night".

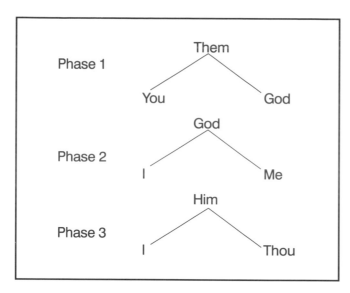

Fig. 1: Laestadian congregation: Interlocutory notation.

Phase 2: In the place of the "you" by which the clergy address one, the preachers introduce a self-reflexive relation between "I" and "me". This helps each to think about himself, instead of leaving it to "them" (the clergy) to measure his or her conduct by their criteria. So in the place of talk about Nicodemuses, the congregation is told about Ananias who helped Saul change into Paul.

Phase 3: Here one advances beyond the individual's self-awareness (I/me) towards an awareness of co-identity with each other: A congregational realization of self. It is the I/Thou relationship of Martin Buber in which "I encounter you as another I". It is reached through ecstatic confession – open confession on the floor of the congregation.

In the fjordal community where I lived, it was really only at this climactic conclusion to the congregational meetings that I heard these Saami openly and joyously acknowledge themselves, to each other, as Saami:

"Mii ibmel mannat ... Mii sabmelazzat!" (Paine 1988a:2-26).

For a congregation that does *not* "do", its achievements are considerable. Paraphrased they are these two:

1. Justification of the hard conditions of life within the local community.

2. A myth of universality of which the local community is the centre and which is maintained independently of the Church and State (Paine 1988b:166).

This trail of self-consciousness tails off in *my* account of Saami self-consciousness – my fieldwork shifted over to the reindeer pastoralists, and still later, to the new ethnopolitics that began emerging in the late 60s. However, the Laestadian congregation, while no longer the sole focus of collective self-consciousness, remains an enduring presence in many Saami communities (see Björklund 1978, Nystö 1982, Steinlien 1984, Torp 1986).

Ludic Bridges: 1

I remember – from when I lived on the coast in the village of Kokelv[7] in the 50s – the disapproval and disparagement metred out, self-righteously, to young women of the village who 'dressed up' (in clothes bought through catalogue orders) before taking the steamer to Hammerfest – the regional centre of Norwegian culture and urban life. Once in Hammerfest, the girls, we believed, would do their best to hide their Saami identity. In the village, they were called *riw'go* – the Saami word for a non-Saami woman.

Today in Kokelv, there is a *Saami Saervi* (association), a building housing a small museum, and on festive occasions there will be young people who 'dress up' in a Saami *gak'te/kofte* (dress)!

Nowhere along the coast, in the 50s, did one hear the Saami *joik* (('folk' ballad) Arnberg *et al.* 1969): Forbidden by the Laestadians as the noise of the devil, associated with drunkenness and debauchery, it was also *derided*, by Saami and Norwegians alike, as "primitive". By the 70s, the *joik* had been 're-discovered', and not just by ethnomusicologists but by young Saami who gave it a Country & Western flavour! There were concerts, there were records – they went up near the top of the charts in Norway. One *joik* composition, suitably adapted, was Norway's entry in a Euro-competition.

In 1968 NSR *(Norske Samers Riksforbund/ Norga Samiid Riikasaer'vi)* was established.[8] Its mandate was to take care of Saami interests on the basis of "Saami premises". Something of the 'watershed' nature of this move may be appreciated by contrastning it with the bitter cynicism of Per Foxtad, *the* Saami nationalist in Norway of an earlier generation: "You can certainly be Saami" he said, "if you learn to speak Norwegian properly, if you wear Norwegian clothes, if you adopt Norwegian customs – then you will have no difficulties" (Dahl 1970: 12). Ten years later, NSR voted *not* to send a representative to the celebrations honouring King Olav's 75th birthday. Meanwhile, in 1973 the Nordic Saami Institute/*Sami Instituhtta* (NSI) was opened in Kautokeino with a mandate to conduct research on "Saami premises" – meaning that it takes a Saami to understand Saami culture and the circumstances in which Saami find themselves.[9] Also in 1973, the 7th Nordic Ethnographical Congress/*Nordiske etnografiske möte* was held in Tromsö with *"Samfunnsforskning og minoritetssamfunn"* as its theme – one of the plenary speakers was Alf Isak Keskitalo who was about to take up an appointment with NSI.

He spoke, he said, as a "minority representative at the complementary majority's congress" (Keskitalo 1976: 18). He had some hard words. Even minority participation in research, he said, upholds "a very subtle form of majority-minority relationship with a nearly oppressive function" (p. 20). And in respect to the people who are researched, "majority scientists tend to fix attention on the more archaic aspects of the minority group, and thus underestimate its complexity and differentiation" (p. 20). Most striking of all, though, was his statement as to why he chose to speak, not his native Saami ("unintelligible to most of you") nor in Norwegian, the majority language, but in English. To speak in Norwegian would be to subscribe to the "linguistic asymmetry" – a characteristic of majority-minority relations – even while speaking out against that asymmetry, thereby reducing all that he had to say to "nothing but a word game" (p. 16).

Another 'ludic' case-history that I should present briefly is about team A's work in relation to the ideology of team B; it is a 'reciprocal' of the Keskitalo one. Team A members (the non-Saami academics) are likely to think – or wish to think – that their research is 'objective' and 'truthful' and as such cannot bring harm to its subjects. (But this does not stop us making claims in the opposite direction: That our research may help its subjects.) Team B, however, will, in circumstances relating to their *own* position, denounce the 'objectivity' as a sham and as damaging to their people; but as their circumstances change, so may, quite radically, what they say about some piece of team A research. My case in point is the research – the research career, really – of Harald Eidheim: Norwegian social anthropologist and the most important member of team A.

Eidheim has sought to understand how Saami cope with the "stigma of inferiority" – especially evident along the coast – in relation to Norwegian-speakers and Norwegian culture. The central questions have been: How do coastal Saami live with the stigma? How do Saami activists – team B, NSR leadership, members of NSI – grapple with the problem? He has reflected over the dilemma of the activists (in "the Lappish movement"): The more they pressed their programme, the greater the resistance they encountered among many of their own people.

"The traditional rejection of Lappish identity by Norwegians has deposited a stigma of inferiority in the Lappish population, which in some areas overrules all new moral principles advocated by the leaders of the movement and prevents a positive response" (Eidheim 1971a: 7).

Here I would draw attention to a couple of acknowledgments that Eidheim makes:

"During my fieldwork I have enjoyed the hospitality of many people who in various ways have exposed their private dilemmas of identity to me" (p. 8).

And he thanks Saami activists

"who have taken me into their confidence and introduced me to their political backstage – a position from which I have been able to gather much valuable information" (p. 8).

Of entering a coastal Saami village, he writes: "I knew, of course, that I was on the edges of the Lappish area, but my eyes and ears told me that I was inside a Norwegian fjordal community" (1971b: 52). After a while, though, he 'discovered' that Lappish was the domestic language in most households but that it functioned as "a secret language or code, regularly used only in situations where trusted Lappish identities are involved" (p. 55). Eventually, they "became more careless with the 'secret'" (it helped that he could enter into simple conversations in Saami). It was at this point that people whom he had come to know best in the village "started admitting me their personal dilemmas of identity. This would often take the form of confessions: They were after all a kind of Lapp" (pp. 54, 55).

What did team B make of all this – of the "secret" and the sharing it with a Norwegian ethnographer? The fieldwork was done in the early 60s, and by the time of Keskitalo's speech to the 7th Nordic Ethnografic Congress, in 1973, team B members would say (to me, and I am sure to others) "There'd be no stigma if Eidheim hadn't invented it!" In short, non-Saami ethnographers' habit of collecting 'dirt' about our people, our culture, injures us. But by the 80s, things had changed on all fronts. So that just as the fjordal villagers had earlier drawn comfort from sharing their secret with that sympathetic stranger in their midst, NSR leadership now began to seek his thoughts about strategy on the ethnopolitical front. Eidheim, now "Harald", sitting in Oslo for the most part, became a conduit of information and contacts. He wrote about the cause of NSR in the newspapers; he attended (sometimes arranging) meetings with parliamentarians; and so forth. The ethnographer of team A became a resource person for team B.

Ludic Bridges: 2

In the 50s and 60s when I was attached to various pastoral camps, the interface between Saami and non-Saami identity (in the Saami pastoralist view of the matter) was expressed less around language policy, pasturing rights, and such like (which is not to say these were not important issues) and more around the reindeer:

"When it comes to our animals, each of us is his own boss. ... everyone of us wants his herd to grow – there's the motivation for our hard way of life" (Paine 1987: 7, 13).

What also belongs to this familiar proposition – of the reindeer as a key or summarizing symbol – are the expressions of Saami-ness attached to the *utilization* of reindeer products. Consider the following scenario. Ellon Ailu had sold a dozen animals alive to the Kautokeino Co-operative; so as we return to the winter pastures, he had a wad of banknotes tucked away inside his heavy winter clothing, and that is all:

"On cue, as we entered the cabin, the women looked askance at the money and began hectoring Ellon Ailu:

'Where's the tallow? the blood? the intestinal lining? the heart? the tongue? the head and the marrow bones?' They weren't even mentioning the better joints of meat; and they hadn't finished yet: 'Where are the skins for the clothing we all wear? And the sinew for the sewing of that clothing?'" (Paine 1987: 3).

This was no isolated instance.

Arising from all this are a couple of insistent claims: Only "we Saami" understand reindeer (non-Saami cannot possibly understand what this means to us) and only "we Saami" know how to utilize properly its different products.

For the pastoralists, "you are what you eat" is a truism enwrapping their culture. But at all points – *when* an animal should be slaughtered and *how*, and *how* the meat should be prepared – the Norwegian market opposed Saami praxis. The rub for the Saami was, of course, that they had also to sell *their* meat as a market product. Here it must suffice to say that the market demands lean meat whereas Saami, still today, 'celebrate' (I would like to say) the *fatness* of their meat.[10]

Today, though, self-conscious talk – anguished talk – about the quality of reindeer meat is side-lined as the pastoralists find that control of *access to the pastoral life itself* has been lost: Norwegian law now determines how many, and who among them, will continue as pastoralists, and how many animals they may have. The law (*lov om reindrift*) came into force in 1976.[11]

Then in 1979 an *ad hoc* group of seven young Saami – they called themselves the Saami Action Group (SAG) – put up a *lavvo* (tent) outside Parliament, on that piece of grass with the hallowed name of Eidsvollsplass. They declared that they would stay put and keep a hunger-strike until Parliament rescinded its authorization for the damming of the Alta River, flowing though ancestral Saami lands. The dam threatened reindeer pastures as well as the tundra ecology/economy of the village of Masi (Paine 1982).

What I want to stress here is, first, the significance of the SAG event, and second, its ludic properties:

"*...instead of shaping themselves to the politically dominant reality – to the world outside them – the strikers shaped it to themselves, and they attained their reality in the very act of portraying it*" (Paine 1985a: 201).

"*...by expressing reality as they saw it, the strikers led many Norwegians to rearrange their own experience concerning their nation*" (p. 201).

"*/The effect/ was to place two new and troubling questions on the Norwegian political agenda: 'Who are Saami? What are Saami rights?' The important thing about these questions is that they implicitly assert: 'There are and will be Saami! There are special Saami rights!' These questions superseded the traditional Norwegian question...: 'Why should anyone wish to remain a "Lapp"'* (p. 228).

In denoting the hunger strike as drama, I am separating it from everyday reality – *and make-believe was im-*

portant to the impact that SAG achieved. Those seven momentarily became "the Saami" and their *lavvo* the summarizing symbol of Saami culture. A similar political mission has been recognized for carnivals (Manning 1983), but carnivals are set apart in time and space from other activities. SAG, by contrast, "*usurped*" time and place and *intruded,* unbidden and unheralded, upon the routines, consciences and, above all, the imaginations of the citizens and politicians of Oslo – and eventually of the whole country" (Paine 1985a: 227).

But exactly on account of its 'playfulness', this kind of behaviour arouses disquiet, apprehension, suspicion among many Saami, and the hostility of some. It is strange and rather offensive behaviour, far removed from the 'traditional'; many "would rather continue in the game of survival without trying to roll the dice" (Anderson 1982: 109).

Others asked *whose* "Saami premises" are being activated? NSR, for example, was seen as romanticising the reindeer pastoral minority among the Saami population, as presenting them as *the* standard bearer for *the* true Saami culture. Whereas – the contrary view was – these nomads are really an anachronism in the modern world. If they represent Saami culture, some would say, we can no longer regard ourselves as Saami. Little wonder, then, that the hunger-strikers – in Oslo of all places, with their *lavvo* of all things! – provoked a strident backlash in some Saami circles in the north.

In short, it is the team B dilemma (seen also in the case of Alf Isak Keskitalo). Committed to Saami expressions of self-consciousness, they elevate their own experiences (and interpretations thereof) as though they are shared by all Saami; but the painful truth, at the moment, is that among themselves Saami claim different experiences, or where one might suppose that experiences are similar, there are very likely to be markedly different interpretations. This is particularly troubling when working for a consensual *political* Saami front (below).

Recently, another kind of crisis was visited upon the pastoralists: 'Chernobyl' (Paine 1987a; 1989). The accident provoked different Saami voices. Sometimes it was talked about in terms of *metameaning* and final causes:

'Chernobyl' *encodes a message about social Darwinism.* 'Chernobyl' *is cited as evidence for the demise of Saami culture; in particular, the disappearance of reindeer pastoralism in an agricultural come industrial world. And Saami sometimes add, that in the view of many non-Saami, the demise is overdue. The media, in attempts to keep* 'Chernobyl' *newsworthy, also portrayed it in such metameaningful terms. But the media never said what some Saami know subjectively and say –that* 'we Saami are outlawed people' *(a South Saami), that* 'we realize that we don't count for much' *(a North Saami).* 'Chernobyl' *in other words, has not just remained an accident for the Saami but has become, for many, an em-*

bodiment of history, cropping up in conversations, from time to time, linked to other happenings in Saami non-Saami relations (Paine 1989: 141).

At other times I would hear it talked about in terms of *stigmatization*: Reindeer meat, their "quality product" they call it, was rendered unclean: However, dramatic differences in degree of radiation of pastures and animals undermined solidarity in the face of adversity. Radiation in the South Saami areas was exponentially higher than among the North Saami – in places as much as ten times more. This difference predisposed the North and South to different 'Chernobyl' strategies with respect to the all-important domestic market for reindeer meat. The North wished the government to raise the radiation limit enough to free their[12] meat for the market. This was done. But it was of no help to the pastoralists of the South. Worse than no help, they argued that making an exception of reindeer meat in this way *added* to the stigmatization factor: What housewife, they argued, would buy reindeer meat when this means risking more contamination than with any other meat? It would be better to withdraw all reindeer meat from the market until such time as its radiation falls to the level of other household meats. The bitterness of the South Saami, a small minority within a minority, was directed less to the government than to their own northern-dominated national association of Saami reindeer owners (Norske Reindriftsamers Landsforbund/ *Norgga Boazosapmelaccaid Riikasearvi*)

Once again, then, I had to put away any idea of mobilization of solidarity on the basis of simply being Saami (1987:154f.). Moreover, fieldwork at that time in one of the worst contaminated South Saami districts, confirmed how each family made their own decisions as how best to cope. A memorandum sent to a government department demanded that: "Individual solutions be accepted". This may strike others as an inefficient, ultimately dangerous, way of tackling a catastrophe such as 'Chernobyl', but it is consonant with all that we know about Saami (and other) pastoral society and culture. Consider: No hierarchy, discretional authority, easily divisible capital with anticipatory inheritance – always in ecologic circumstances uncertainty.

Nation-Association

The foregoing belong to the temper and circumstances in which the goal – admittedly but one of a series, but a symbolic benchmark – of a Saami parliament was achieved this year (after a long struggle). The NSR programme is built around four principal demands: (1) The Saami people be mentioned in the Norwegian constitution; (2) there be a Saami elected assembly; (3) Saami becomes a second official language in areas of Saami concentration; and (4) Saami usufruct –

where practiced from time immemorial – be accepted as having bestowed "ownership".

In 1979, a dissenter group broke with NSR, charging that its leadership was elitist and radical. Two aggravations stand out in particular: Embracement of the pastoral nomad as the symbol of Saami culture and the deliberate distancing from the symbol of the Norwegian crown.

The dissenters founded SLF (*Samenes Landsforbund/Sami Aednamsaervi*). It was to provide a "non-ideological" alternative to NSR whose demands (in the SLFers' view) constitute a cultural regression, a "going back" to a condition that Saami had "left behind".

"/We/ honour and respect the constitution, the king and his government, parliament and other official authorities" (Sagat 1-1-80).

"What rights do Saami lack today? ... It is difficult to suppose that any so-called 'special rights' would be an improvement over what we already have in our democracy" (SLF 1979: 1).

So NSR and SLF are alternatives about *culture* and the alternatives are politicized in terms of relationships to the nation-state. SLF says that Saami have obtained "equality" (*likhet*) with Norwegians and should not be allowed to enjoy the rewards of their Norwegianization. But, say NSR, this would ensure the demise of Saami culture, we must strive for recognition of "equal worth" (*likeverd*) – if semantics are any witness, "politics" have been unleashed!

It is important to note that the NSR-SLF difference is as much about Norwegian culture as it is about Saami culture. The SLF people have learned a new culture (Norwegian) and are enjoying it. For the most part they are farmers and fjordal fishermen; some of them are drawn into *kommune* or *fylke* (as opposed to national) politics – that is to say, they enjoy active membership in one or another Norwegian political party. This is a larger world than the Saami one they knew, and altogether more challenging and rewarding. They belong to a new Saami *petit bourgeoisie*. Yet it is among the NSR that one finds the greater competence in and appreciation of the intellectual domains of Norwegian culture (tertiary levels of education among them is not uncommon) – and they put this competence to polemical use against the threat of 'Norwegianization' that still faces Saami culture.

The NSR leadership enjoys the transnational participation in Fourth World affairs – and it is the NSR that catches the imagination and enthusiasm of team A anthropologists. SLF have been ignored when not derided. Why? First of all, I see no cause for surprise – anthropology's reflexes lead it to the NSR camp (and to 'working relationships' between some – but not all – team A and team B members). Both the NSR and much of anthropology are committed to "value culture" (Kroeber) – indeed, it is their principal resource. Thus 'the culture of the Saami' is a shibboleth; the oneness or wholeness implied in a phrase such as "the Saami" is assumed where it should be demonstrated.

On the other hand, I believe that, among other messages, what SLFers are saying to us (team A and much of NSR leadership) is: "You 'university overclass' may call us Saami, but we're not – not any longer!" In other words, they are talking about cultural succession: Of a culture that is no longer 'real' for them being replaced by another.[13] The SLF message is, I agree with Ingold (pers. comm.), also one of rejecting cultural power brokerage: "By calling us Saami, you are asserting symbolic control over us; you are saying that we are still in your bailiwick, that you 'own' us as subjects, to be studied, defended, patronized. We don't need this!"[14]

I hope I have now said enough (much had to be left unsaid) to suggest how Saami engagement in issues pertaining to 'self as nation' is one of *doing* and of *division* (not of being and unity).

The NSR-SLF battle[15] was heated up by acute awareness of the fact that the Saami Rights Commission/*Samerettsutvalget* had a mandate to prepare broad recommendations to Parliament. The Commission was established in 1980 as a direct consequence of the hunger strike the year before.

The NSR-SLF controversy was taken into the Commission itself. It started even over Commission membership: To the displeasure of NSR who saw themselves as the only legitimate representative of Saami rights, there was SLF membership as well as NSR. Nor could NSR understand why national associations such as the Norwegian Farmers' Association were afforded places on the Commission:[16] The presence of *Norwegian* associations is prejudicial to Saami rights, they argued. The answer to this was clear for SLF: Many Saami are farmers. For their part, SLF objected to the inclusion of the Association of Saami Reindeer Owners for, they argued, it is but a small minority of Saami who follow that livelihood!

So the work of the Commission continually ran into obstacles. But when votes were counted, the "NSR" side could muster sufficient to carry the day. The first volume of the Commission's findings appeared in '84; something of an anti-climax, it recommended a clause in the constitution and a Saami parliament – but land rights were held over to the next volume (which has yet to appear). But NSR had to make concessions: the Saami "parliament" is to be an advisory body, they had wished for more.[17]

Parliament ratified the recommendations in '87.[18] Before elections to the Saami parliament could be held, there had to be a national census (*mantallsliste*) of self-declared Saami. Forecasters expected five thousand would register – perhaps one in five or one in six across the country who were eligible (on basis of par-

entage/grandparentage); and 5.500 did. There was some anxiety about what the turn out would be like. Norwegian newspaper comment veered between the bored and the halfamused. Along with Karasjok and Kautokeino, Oslo registered the most Saami. Informed opinion is that many Saami adopted a cautious pragmatic 'wait & see' policy towards this new creature – a Saami parliament.

There followed party campaigns, sponsoring candidates for the 39 seats distributed between 13 regional constituencies. NSR ran a list as did several of the Norwegian political parties. And there were threatened boycotts: The association of Saami Reindeer Owners, arguing their special interest, would declare a boycott should they be denied some reserved seats of their own: They were denied and their boycott was not effective, as far as I know. SLF became divided among themselves; the leadership urged members to boycott the whole proceedings, out of first principles. However, King Olav's acceptance of an invitation to attend the ceremonial opening of the parliament had them scrambling to attend the ceremony!

Voters' turn-out was 75% (of the 5.500). NSR received 35% of the poll and 18 seats, *Arbeiderparti* 20% and 7 seats. Apparently there was little difference between their election platforms. Among the variety of smaller parties making up the balance, several look like NSR satellites. Thirteen women won seats (exactly one third of the total).

Elected as the Saami parliament's first president was Ole Henrik Magga – a prominent member of team B, he had been Chairman of NSR during the period of the hunger strike and the ensuing confrontations with the government; also, he recently assumed the Chair of Finno-Ugric Studies at Oslo after Knut Bergsland (while continuing as one of the research directors of the *Sami Instituhtta* in Kautokeino).

...but events have run ahead of analysis!

Notes

1. For a good overview, see Vorren and Manker (1958 in Norwegian, 1962 in English).
2. But see Aubert 1978.
3. And by visual artists and musicians; Kaalund (1986) provides an introductory account of Saami painters and sculptors, together with Greenlandic artists.
4. The published proceedings are important source books along with *Sami Aellin/Sameliv*, a Yearbook published in Norway. The first five of the Nordic Saami Conferences (1953-62) were published in English (Hill ed. 1960; Hill & Nickul eds. 1969) as well as in Finnish, Norwegian and Swedish. Today, effort is made to provide a Saami language version of conferences.
5. For instance, see Ruong 1964.
6. Try Briggs (1970 and 1982) if you want that; and see Cohen (1989) on the self-consciousness of the anthropologist.
7. The village and my presence in it, is featured in Nielsen (1986).
8. Stordahl 1982 is an essay on its emergence.
9. NSI publishes research papers in its series *Diedut*.
10. More on this is to be found in Paine 1987b.
11. See *Landbruksdepartementet* 1976; further to issues raised here, see Björklund 1988.

12. Particularly devastating is the pollution of saami foods – reindeer meat, freshwater fish, berries.
13. Kroeber distinguishes between "value culture" and "reality culture" – I suggest it is the latter the SLF would embrace. For discussion of Kroeber's terms, see Wolf 1982.
14. Ingold's construal (pers. comm.). Cognate to the present discussion of NSR and SLF is Ingold's on "minority-culture ideology" of "local elites" among the Skolt Saami of northern Finland (Ingold 1976: 245-53).
15. A fuller account is given in Paine 1990; and as a conflict in terms of Fourth World ideology, see Paine 1985b.
16. But it is Norwegian practice for all commissions to have broad representation of professional/occupational interests.
17. NOU 1984 is the full text of the Commission's first volume, a seventy page English summary is also available (Ministry of Justice); Eidheim 1985 is a critique of the Commission report by several Norwegian anthropologists.
18. See *Justis- og politidepartementet* 1984.

References

Anderson, Myrdene 1982. "Vectors of diversification and specialization ation in Saami society". In: Vinson H.Sutlive et al. (eds.), *Contemporary Nomadic and Pastoral Peoples: Asia and the North.* Williamsburg, Virginia: College of William & Mary, Dept. of Anthropology.

Arnberg, Matts et al. 1969. *Jojk/ Yoik.* Stockholm: Sveriges Radios Forlag.

Aubert, Wilhelm 1978. *Den samiske befolkning i Nord-Norge.* Oslo: Statistisk sentralbyrå, nr. 107.

Björklund, Ivar 1978. *Kvaen-Same-Norsk: En sosialantropologisk analyse av 'De tre stammers möte'.* Tromsö: Universitetet i Tromsö.

Björklund, Ivar 1988. "For mye rein i Finmark?" *Finmark Dagbladet,* 29th December.

Briggs, Jean, L. 1970. *Never in Anger. Portrait of an Eskimo Family.* Harvard University Press.

Briggs, Jean, L. 1982. "Living dangerously: the contradictory foundations ions of value in Canadian Inuit society". In: Eleanor Leacock & Richard Lee (eds.), *Politics and History in Band Societies.* Cambridge University Press.

Baer, Anders Pedersen 1926. "Erindringer 1825-1849." *Norvegia Sacra.*

Cohen, Anthony P. 1989. "Self-conscious anthropology". Paper presented to the ASA Conference, *Anthropology and Autobiography.*

Dahl, Tor Edvin 1970. *Samene i dag og i morgen. En rapport.* Oslo: Gyldendal.

Eidheim, Harald 1971a. "Preface". In: *Aspects of the Lappish Minority Situation.* Oslo: Universitetsforlaget.

Eidheim, Harald 1971b. "When ethnic identity is a social stigma". In: *Aspects of the Lappish Minority Situation.* Oslo: Universitetsforlaget.

Eidheim, Harald et al. 1985. "Samenes rettsstilling: likeverd, velferd og rettferdighet". *Nytt Norsk Tidsskrift, Nr. 2.*

Hill, Rowland G.P. (ed.) 1960. *The Lapps Today, I.* Paris: Mouton.

Hill, Rowland G.P. & Karl Nickul (eds.) 1969. *The Lapps Today, II.* Oslo: Universitetsforlaget.

Ingold, Tim 1976. *The Skolt Lapps Today.* Cambridge University Press.

Justis- og politidepartementet 1987. *Om lov om Sametinget og andre samiske rettsforhold (Sameloven).* Oslo (Ot. prp. nr. 33).

Kaalund, Bodil 1986. "Greenland and Sapmi". In: Torsten Blöndal (ed.), *Northern Poles.* Copenhagen: Blöndal.

Keskitalo, Alf Isak 1976. "Research as an inter-ethnic relation". Tromsö Museum: *Acta Boreali B Humaniora, Nr. 13.*

Landbruksdepartementet 1976. *Om lov om reindrift.* Oslo (Ot. prp. nr. 9).

Larsen, Anders 1912. *Baeivve-Alggo.* Kristiania: Private Publisher.

Manning, Frank 1983. "Text, strategy and celebration". In: Frank Manning (ed.), *Bread and Circuses. Festivity and Public Performance in Contemporary Societies.* Ohio: Bowling Green University Popular Press.

Nielsen, Reidar 1986. *Folk uten fortid.* Oslo: Gyldendal.

NOU 1984. *Om Samenes rettsstilling.* (NOU 1984: 18). Oslo: Universitetsforlaget.

Nysto, S.R. 1982. *Etnisitet og religiösitet – to uforenelige statuskombinasjoner i etnopolitisk mobilisering?* Tromsö: Universitetet i Tromsö.

Paine, Robert 1982. *Dam a River, Damn a People?* Copenhagen: IWGIA.

– 1985a. "Ethnodrama & the 'fourth world': The Saami action group in Norway, 1979-81". In: Noel Dyck (ed.), *Indigenous Peoples and The Nation-State.* St. John's: Memorial University, Institute of Social and Economic Research.

– 1985b. "The claim of the fourth world". In: Jens Brøsted et al (eds.), *Native Power.* Oslo: Universitetsforlaget.

– 1987a. "Accidents, ideologies and routines: 'Chernobyl' over Norway". *Anthropology Today,* 3(4).

– 1987b. "Reindeer meat and Saami culture". (unpubl. ms.).

– 1988a. "The persuasions of 'being' and 'doing': An ethnographic essay". *International Journal of Moral and Social Studies,* 3(1).

– 1988b. "Grace out of stigma: the cultural self-management of a Saami congregation". *Ethnologia Europaea XVIII.*

– 1989. "Making the invisibla 'visible': Coming to terms with 'Chernobyl' & its experts, a Saami illustration". *International Journal of Moral and Social Studies,* 4(2).

– 1990. "The claim of aboriginality: Saami in Norway". In: Reidar Grönhaug et al. (eds.), *Festskrift to Fredrik Barth* (in press).

Pirak, A. 1933. *En nomad och hans liv.* Stockholm (Saami version in 1937).

Ruong, Israel 1964. *Jåhkåkaska sameby.* Svenska Landsmål och Svenskt Folkliv.

Skum, Nils Nilsson 1955. *Valla renar.* Stockholm: Gebers.

Steinlien, Öystein 1984. *Kulturel endring og etnisk kontinuitet.* Tromsö: Universitetet i Tromsö.

Stordahl, Vigdis 1982. *'Samer sier nei til kongen?'* Tromsö: Universitetet i Tromsö.

Torp, Eivind 1986. *Fra 'Markafinn' til Same. Etnopolitisk mobilisering i en laestadiansk kontekst.* Tromsö: Universitetet i Tromsö.

Turi, Johan 1910. *Muittalus samid birra* (edited and translated into Danish by Emilie Demant Hatt). English edition 1931: *Turi's Book of Lappland.* London: Jonathan Cape.

Utsi, Paulus 1975. *Giela Giela.* Uppsala: Almqvist & Wiksell.

Valkeapää, Nils Aslak 1974. *Gita ijat cuov'gadat.* Oulus: publ. by the author.

Vorren, Örnulv & Ernest Manker 1958. *Samekulturen. En oversikt.* Tromsö: Tromsö Museum. English edition 1962: *Lapp Life and Customs. A Survey.* Oslo University Press and Oxford University Press.

Wolf, Eric R. 1982. "Culture: panacea or problem?" *Northeastern Anthropological Newsletter ,* Fall.

Between Global and Local Politics:

The dilemma of Greenlandic Home Rule

Mads Fægteborg

ABSTRACT

How can it be that Greenlandic Home Rule, which has no decisive influence on foreign and security policy, on the one hand is participating in the power-games of the superpowers and on the other hand, is anti-militaristic? In this presentation, the author gives some brief examples of the growing dilemma Greenland faces. Unfortunately, the lack of sources – particularly the minutes from the Greenland Parliament (Lagting), which have not been published since 1984 – sometimes leaves the author in a position where he is solely dependent on less reliable press reports.

The most recent history

October 2, 1972 was the day when 70.3% of the given votes in Greenland were cast against joining the EEC. Unlike the Faroe Islands, Greenland had no Home Rule arrangement and as a consequence, had to follow Denmark into the EEC.[1]

The result of the plebiscite made then Member of the Danish Parliament, Moses Olsen, elected in Greenland, declare in the Parliament that it probably would be the proper time to take the necessary steps for a poll in favour of a changed relationship to Denmark.[2]

In Denmark many misunderstood the message and thought that Moses Olsen was espousing ideas of a separate Greenland. That was not the case, but he had started a chain of reactions beginning with the setting up of the Home Rule Committee in January 1973[3], followed by the Home Rule Commission in October 1975.[4] As is probably known, the Commission recommended Home Rule for Greenland. After a plebiscite in Greenland, the bill governing Greenland's Home Rule (Law no. 56 of February 21, 1979) was passed. Home Rule was introduced in Greenland on May 1, 1979.

Law no. 56

In § 11, sec. 1 of the bill governing Greenland's Home Rule it is stated that,

"The Danish Government has the decisive word in questions concerning relations with foreign countries." In § 10, sec. 1 of the same bill it is stated that, *"The Home Rule Government is subjected to the obligations toward treaties and other international rules which at any time are binding for the nation."* Additionally, § 10, sec. 2 states that, *"The Home*

Rule authorities are at any time limited by the authorities that are delegated to international organisations, in accordance with § 20 in the Constitution."

Furthermore, § 12 and 13 stipulate that laws, administrative regulations or treaties which concern Greenland and/or are of particular interest to Greenland have to be presented to the Greenlandic Home Rule for comments prior to presentation in the Danish Folketing (parliament) and prior to publication, ratification and agreement. According to § 13, sec. 1, the Home Rule authorities are to present their comments within 6 months after receipt.

"If, because of compelling circumstances, the presentation has not been possible, the law, administrative regulation or treaty has to be presented as soon as possible for comments by Home Rule bodies"

in accordance with § 14, sec. 2.[5]

In more informal language, it means that Greenland cannot conduct independent foreign and security policy. But at the same time, it means that issues of particular interest can be taken up for negotiations within the United Realm.

The EEC

Greenland, as is known, withdrew from the EEC in February 1985. The withdrawal was the first appearance in international politics of Home Rule. Locally in Greenland there were disagreements on which policy one should conduct towards the EEC. It is not possible within the limits of this presentation to focus on these disagreements, which is why I confine myself to dealing with the policy actually conducted by the Home Rule government, *i.e.*, the policy of the governing party, *Siumut*.

But why did Greenland want to leave the EEC? Former member of the European Parliament, Finn Lynge (*Siumut*), has endeavoured to reduce the whole matter into three headings, "the EEC issue was a question of resource control, of national identity and of attitudes toward authorities."[6] Neither geographically, ethnically nor culturally is Greenland a part of Europe, Finn Lynge wrote prior to the plebiscite and he saw Greenland's membership as having three advantages solely for the EEC: 1) access to one of the largest storerooms of fish, 2) access to minerals in a long-term perspective, and 3) security reasons. Obviously, some circles were worried that the struggle against the EEC could turn out to be a struggle against NATO as well.[7]

Greenlanders went to the ballot boxes on February 23, 1982. The result was 53% of the given votes in favour of leaving the EEC.[8] In February 1985 the withdrawal was executed.

The President of the Home Rule Government (Landsstyreformand) Jonathan Motzfeldt pointed out, following the end of the debate in the Landsting that:

"The most important experience we have gained during these discussions, and which fully justifies our decision to withdraw is the fact of how incredibly difficult it is to understand each other across the Atlantic. Coherence and demands which we consider quite natural and reasonable are received in Brussels with consternation, scepticism and aversion because the Europeans do not immediately grasp what goes on up here. It may strike you as banal but this comprehensibility gap has been the most difficult problem to overcome during the entire process. When, finally, we succeeded in convincing nine European countries to support our case, this was only a result of a strenuous and time-consuming process on the part of Greenland and Denmark during the negotiations with the EEC."[9]

Security policy is outside the EEC mandate and consequently Greenland's security policy was not touched on during the withdrawal negotiations. Nevertheless, according to anonymous sources inside the Danish Ministry of Foreign Affairs, it was precisely the deliberations about security policies that resulted in a favourable agreement of withdrawal for Greenland.[10] The agreement meant great economic advantages for Greenland through a fishing agreement with the EEC. Even if the withdrawal agreement had been disadvantageous for Greenland, Greenlandic politicians, with full support from Denmark, would have been in favour of a unilateral withdrawal. This would no doubt have led to Greenland inviting tenders for fishing rights in Greenlandic waters. Unquestionably, this would have been of no small interest for – among others – East German and Soviet trawlers. Before the introduction of Home Rule, the USSR had shown great interest in fishing in Greenland as well, offering Greenland fishing factories of Soviet design, including training for Greenlandic workers. That was hardly offered for fishing policy reasons alone.[11]

History has shown us that standing outside the EEC has been more profitable to Greenland than being within it. But this was not a given fact at the time when the Landsting had to approve the results of the negotiations. Following an amendment to the order of business enabling elections to be held in addition to the statutory each fourth year, *Inuit Ataqatigiit* and *Atassut* gave the governing *Siumut* a vote of no-confidence in March 1984. *Atassut* did not want to leave the EEC. *Inuit Ataqatigiit* found that *Siumut* had made overly large concessions to the EEC.[12]

Party programmes

Siumut adopted their party programme in July 1977. In their programme one can read the following regarding foreign policy:

"We stand by our no to the EEC", and *"Denmark's foreign commitments which are in force at the time of the introduction of Home Rule shall not automatically apply to our country, but be negotiated between the (Danish) government and the Landsstyre to attain an agreement about how and in what way these will apply to our country"*, and *"Siumut supports the recently created united Inuit organisation, Inuit Circumpolar Conference (ICC) in all its endeavours and purposes."*

Inuit Ataqatigiit adopted their party programme in November 1978. Their main objectives are: "On the basis of anti-imperialism to fight colonialism and the neocolonial development in all its aspects. With this in mind, to work for recognition of the collective ownership by the indigenous peoples of *Kalaallit Nunaat* (Greenland) and as a nation with full sovereignty over their own country."

Atassut published their programme in January 1977. Regarding their position towards the outside world it says, "Recognising that all the countries of the world are dependent on each other, and that it is impossible for Greenland to isolate itself from the outside world, Greenland must live in an open relationship with other nations based on the attitude that all peoples are equal."[13]

Preliminary conclusions

Regarding the politics conducted towards the EEC, the political parties followed their party programmes. *Siumut* and *Inuit Ataqatigiit* wanted to withdraw from the EEC, *Atassut* were in favour of staying within.

Of course, human resources are limited in a country with only some fifty thousand inhabitants. This fact created a dilemma in the actual policy conducted. Many resources were set aside to deal with the EEC-issue, consequently local issues were paid less attention to than actually merited. The chairman of the Landstyre fully agreed when he wrote in a newspaper article in 1982, "It has been a lot of work to build up a completely new administration within Home Rule, and we have done quite a lot of travelling within the Landsstyre. Not as many trips to Sydprøven or to Upernavik as could have been wished, but instead many trips to Copenhagen, to Bonn, to Brussels and to Strasbourg."[14]

At the time the Landsting had to debate the agreement reached with the EEC, a peculiar situation arose. As mentioned earlier, *Inuit Ataqatigiit* supported by *Atassut* gave the governing *Siumut* party a vote of no-confidence. A new electoral law was passed and an election was called. Before that, the EEC-agreement was debated. *Inuit Ataqatigiit* voted against the agreement. *Siumut* and *Atassut* voted for the agreement. The peculiar situation was that *Atassut*, which did not want to withdraw from the EEC, and only a few days earlier had been part in the vote of no-confidence, voted in favour of the agreement.[15] Was this an expression of political ambivalence or was it a manoeuvre in seeking more political power after the election?

The first security debates

There is no long tradition in Greenland for discussion on security policy issues. Several factors have had their effect in bringing these issues in focus for discussion and debate during the 1980'ies.

In 1983 in a debate book, *Grønland – Middelhavets Perle* (Greenland – the Mediterranean Pearl) then member of the EEC Parliament, Finn Lynge, and the mayor of Qaqortoq, Henrik Lund (both *Siumut*), introduced their stance concerning war, the military, and the use of force. Henrik Lund writes, among other things, "When one escapes everyday life one cannot convincingly say that the Greenlander has any position on the military. The power game, contrivances of mass destruction and war are, viewed historically, alien to him and are interpreted in the sense that as a civilian member of society, one does not waste time on such things. War as a means of power lies outside everyday life, although you are aware of the use of power between a few individuals but not as a means of war of extermination or as a defense for any convictions." ..."Needless to say, today's Greenlanders are aware of the positions of power in the world. This knowledge, however, does not imply that the world-wide struggle for power such as it is, is readily accepted." ... "In short, we, the Greenlanders, are anti-military. We cannot resign ourselves to attitudes which may lead to the extermination of life which threatens a whole people. We are not part of the 'issue'"...[16]

Finn Lynge enlarged upon why Home Rule is tepid in its interest for the American military activities in the country:

"Among many Greenlanders and certainly among Greenlandic politicians, there is a clear understanding of the important role Greenland plays as far as military strategy is concerned and that this importance is a product of NATO membership and its existing defense treaties. Some are aware of the Monroe Doctrine as well and realise that we are caught in a scheme which has much wider implications outside us and Denmark." – "At the moment, I don't think anyone at all is asking whether the Americans are in Greenland in their own interests or in the interest of the Greenlanders." ... "We consider Greenland part of the NATO alliance."

Finn Lynge continued by pointing out that he did not believe that in the long run Greenland would be able to live with the fact of having no insight or control over the defense areas. He also pointed out, however, that he did not think that this situation would change within a decade. The reasons he gave were partly by referring to the Home Rule Laws and partly the lack of human resources. "Who should control it? Which member of the Home Rule government should we select for it?"[17]

Grønland – Middelhavets Perle spurred an extensive debate as to what kinds of American activities took place in Greenland. It became, however, primarily a debate in the Danish media, in the Folketing and by Danes as a whole. Still, then member of the Folketing, Preben Lange (*Siumut*), contributed to the discussion in February 1983. His concern was whether the installations mentioned in the book were offensive and hence might be subjected to Soviet attack and continued:

"It would mean that yet another thorough investigation would have to be conducted as to whether the Americans respect the agreements signed by the parties to prevent the local population from being subjected to danger and the like in the event of a conflict."[18]

A report regarding the American installations in Greenland was ordered by the Home Rule government (Landsstyre) from the Ministry of Defense. This report was debated in the landsting in October 1983. *Inuit Ataqatigiit* leader and member of Landsting, Aqqaluk Lynge, concluded after the hearing that, "Each time a public debate about the existence of the bases in Greenland takes place, predictably enough, the answer has been that we by no means have the right to interfere, it being a purely Danish/American affair. It would, however, prove illogical to perpetually try to set aside the fact that it concerns a part of our country and disregard what it is being used for. Are we continually to acknowledge that a part of our country is outside our jurisdiction? Are we continually to ignore what is going on in these areas? Aqqaluk Lynge went on to refer to the ICC Resolutions 77-11 and 83-01, among others, both regarding peaceful and safe uses of the Arctic.[19]

This was the first actual debate in the Landsting on matters of security policy and led to the agreement on a resolution which demanded the Landsting be continuously informed in matters of defense. Votes in favour were 18 (*Atassut* and *Siumut*), none against while 6 abstained (*Inuit Ataqatigiit*).[20]

The following year, in November 1984, the Landsting had a debate on nuclear weapons and nuclear power. *Inuit Ataqatigiit*, at that time in a coalition government with *Siumut*, had put the issue on the agenda. A united Landsting closed the debate with a declaration that rejected the stationing of nuclear weapons in Greenland and called for a prohibition against ships and aircrafts armed with nuclear weapons entering Greenlandic territory, both in times of peace and of war.[21]

In 1985, another book concerning the American presence in Greenland, *Thule – fangerfolk og militæranlæg* (Thule – Hunters and Military Installations), was published.[22] The book gave rise to substantial debate in Greenland as it presented a thorough analysis of the co-existence of a military installation and the local indigenous people. The introduction in the book was written by the then president of the Inuit Circumpolar Conference (ICC), presently a member of the Folketing, Hans-Pavia Rosing (*Siumut*). He especially emphasised that:

> "With the introduction of a working group under the auspices of the UN, the Working Group on Indigenous Populations, the so-called Fourth World has made itself known in a decisive and new way. It is precisely in this context that it is of immense importance that the historical discussions regarding our traditional rights are brought forth in a manner that leaves no doubt, thereby forming a sound basis for UN's work on these question."[23]

Essentially, the book was meant as an analysis of the consequences of the Thule Air Base for the local population, rather than as an analysis of the military importance of the base for the strategic games between the superpowers.

The dilemma

Being a co-author of *Thule – fangerfolk og militæranlæg* and later a consultant to the municipality of Thule (Avanersuup Kommunia), I acquired more knowledge of the political game than is usual for a social scientist.

On August 12, 1985, approximately one and a half months after the book had been published, the Landsstyreformand wrote then Minister for Greenlandic Affairs:

> Tom Høyem, "In connection with the publishing of Jens Brøsted and Mads Fægteborg's book Thule – fangerfolk og militæranlæg, I have noticed your statements to the press, and that it seems that the local population have a legitimate claim for compensation, but that it should be the Danish, not the American, state which should pay a possible compensation." ... "In the Home Rule government, we have also read the book mentioned with interest and regard it as an important document in understanding recent Greenlandic history. However, it is the understanding of the Landsstyre that it is doubtful if there is a legal, let alone a moral, existence of a claim for compensation towards those authorities – Danish and American – which in light of those days' political climate were in charge of establishing Thule Air base and

> with it, the removal of the local population from Ummannaq. On the other hand, we think one should establish a relationship between the local population and the base, which would be of future benefit to all parts." ... "In the Home Rule government, we find it will be done best by setting up a US-financed foundation, and a softening of the tight regulations of contact (between the local population and the US personnel) in the defense agreement."[24]

Avanersuup Kommunia wished to be awarded damages. The former ombudsman, Lars Nordskov Nielsen, backed the municipality up on this point of view in a feature article.[25] On September 13, 1985, Avanersuup Kommunia wrote the Landsstyre asking for support in their claim for compensation.[26] Without preceding negotiations with the municipality, Preben Lange announced from the platform in the Folketing in the same wording as the Landsstyreformand that it was doubtful if there really was any basis for a claim for compensation.[27]

Locally in Avanersuup Kommunia all political parties supported the claim. On the national level, the same parties did not fully support the claim. *Siumut*, as already mentioned, did not support the claim. *Inuit Ataqatigiit* supported the claim but did not do anything in the Landsting. *Atassut*, on the other hand, supported the claim in the Folketing.[28] Among other things, the party's representative said, "I will ask the Minister for Greenlandic Affairs to make sure that the case is looked into in depth by the Danish Government before they take an absolute and irrevocable stand. I hope that this issue is not concluded on juridical premises only. The human aspects deserve a thorough investigation. I will ask the Danish Government to consider if it wouldn't be better to form an investigative committee to get the case looked at from all sides in the best way."[29]

Several members of the Folketing were ready to support the demands of the people of Thule but due to the total lack of support on the part of the Landsstyre, the debate gradually diminished. However, the Minister of Greenlandic Affairs, Tom Høyem, took the initiative in a so-called nine point plan to help the Thule people's immediate needs to change its relation to the base. In Greenland, the Landsting was presented with a report about the relationship with the USA. The report was debated in October 1986. Some of Tom Høyem's initiatives were executed at that time, *e.g.*, a radical reduction of 50% of the defence area and an offer to the local people to work on the base as well as an offer for delivery of various consumer goods to the base.[30]

In connection with republishing *Thule – fangerfolk og militæranlæg* in 1987, the Government finally agreed to the Thule people's demands that they set up an investigative committee. This committee has not yet concluded its investigations.

In 1987 the daily paper *Information* provided a number of articles which suggested that the radar installation (LPAR) was contradictory to the ABM agreement. Soviet – and some American – experts were not in doubt. The issue was taken up in the Folketing. In this forum, Preben Lange urged the Danish Government to actively try to speed up the summit meeting between the superpowers regarding the radar installation. Lange, who incidentally was in line with his Danish collaborators, the Social Democratic Party, was heavily criticised by the Landsstyreformand.[31]

Indirectly, *Information*'s articles caused the coalition parties in the government, *Siumut* and *Inuit Ataqatigiit*, to collapse because a member of the government, Aqqaluk Lynge, in an interview to *Information*, had said that Jonathan Motzfeldt had ignored the serious aspects regarding the Thule radar.[32] Apart from this, *Siumut* split in two fractions, one headed by Jonathan Motzfeldt, the other by the party's vice-president (now chairman) Lars Emil Johansen, who was more radical and demanded the forming of an investigative committee having full insight in the political security questions regarding Greenland.[33]

Following the election, a government coalition between *Siumut* and *Inuit Ataqatigiit* was again formed, and after the election to the Folketing, Preben Lange was replaced by Hans-Pavia Rosing. The latter has, *e.g.*, in connection with the debate following Michail Gorbatjov's Murmansk speech, expressed the view that Greenland wanted to support any kind of initiative for detente and de-militarisation.[34]

In 1988 the Landsstyre coalition collapsed again. This time in connection with the election to the Folketing, caused by the security issue, where *Inuit Ataqatigiit*'s candidate Josef Motzfeldt demanded the closure of the American bases.[35]

Finally, in 1988, the foreign and security policy committee was formed, The chairman of the committee, Lars Emil Johansen, realised how little competence the committee had in connection with NATO's possible interest in placing a base at Mestervig in Eastern Greenland. In November 1988, the Minister of Foreign Affairs and the Landsstyreformand together issued a statement about this NATO base. The decision to allow NATO to go ahead with preliminary investigations was immediately criticised by the chairman of the committee, who claimed that the committee should have been heard. The differences of opinion between the Landsstyreformand and the committee, however, were quickly silenced as there was no legal authority for such a hearing.[36]

Lately, we have heard that the Americans want to abandon the Air Base at Søndre Strømfjord and the remaining 3 DYE-stations. The foreign and security committee left for the USA and explained to the Americans that all the US bases in Greenland depended on each other, consequently, if Søndre Strømfjord and the DYE-stations were abandoned, the Americans would have to abandon Thule as well.[37]

Conclusion

One has to realise that today Greenland is making "foreign policy" decisions in a wide range of fields. It is obvious to regard a great part of the fishery policy as foreign policy.

Evidently there were foreign policy aspects involved when the Landsstyreformand demanded in November 1988 that if the Faroe Islands wanted to continue fishing in Greenlandic waters, they had to abide the decision of the United Realm to boycott South Africa and discontinue their fisheries in Namibian waters.[38]

Realistically, one can look at the work of the IVCC as foreign policy if comparing it to the work of the Nordic Council and the West Nordic Parliamentary Liaison Committee.

In wanting Home Rule for Greenland, it was obvious it included greater political independence, which finally was realised in 1979. Parties were formed and opinions for and against the EEC were aired. The cons won the plebiscite and later on, Greenland managed to obtain a fishery agreement with the EEC on good terms.

Since having withdrawn from the EEC in 1985, there has been no further debate of membership or not – it is considered history. On the other hand, much debate continues around the issue of security policy. In summarising, the Landsting generally agrees that Greenland is a nuclear-free territory. Beyond that point, no harmony exists.

In connection with the controversy on security policy, the truth is that factors from outside (scientists, journalists, etc.) often are the ones who raise the row. These public discussions afford a greater awareness of security issues in general, but on the other hand, have also caused internal differences with the *Siumut* party. On the face of it, it might seem the party acts a little taken aback each time a new issue about security policy surfaces. It is a different case with the *Inuit Ataqatigiit*, which has a distinct, anti-militaristic policy, more moderate, however, when in coalition with the *Siumut* than otherwise. *Atassut* is unanimously for the USA and NATO and yet this party has had a far clearer standpoint that the other parties regarding the Thule people's claim.

Siumut, which has been in government since 1979, either alone or in coalition with the *Inuit Ataqatigiit*, and most recently with *Atassut* as a supporting party, has chosen in at least two cases to go against its own supporters, namely by not supporting the Thule people and by refraining from critical views towards the radar at Thule. Both times, even *Siumut* has been more conservative than the Danish Conservative government. The question is then – why? As already mentioned, the question can apparently only be answered by looking at the politicians from the *Siumut* party. The key figures are Jonathan Motzfeldt and Lars Emil

Johansen – together with Moses Olsen promoters of Home Rule and founders of the *Siumut* party.

Jonathan Motzfeldt, who has been in office as Landsstyreformand from the inauguration of the Landsstyre, until now is the paternalistic leader of his country. Internally in the party, he is no longer the absolute leader. Political discussions with *Atassut* leader, Otto Steenholdt following the election to the Landsting in 1987 led to an attempted coup against him. The instigator of the coup was Lars Emil Johansen, but fear of splitting the party in two made it possible for Motzfeldt to continue. But he had to give up his leadership of the party at the party-congress later the same year, a position he had had since the party was established in the 1970'ies besides a short period in 1979-80. Johansen was elected the new leader.[39]

Many public rows between the ideologist Johansen and the pragmatist Motzfeldt might of course, be pleasant reading for those wishing to make use of the political split in the governing party. I cannot quote instances i support of it, but it is a possibility that the Americans have been using the on-going struggle to promote their new strategic policy in Greenland. The fact that the USA have had their bases in Greenland for free through the years seems of little importance today, when they want their presence paid for.

The dilemma facing Greenland's Home Rule government may be more a local phenomenon that a global one. The American bases were established when Greenland was still a Danish colony. In those days, indigenous rights were of less importance than the global game of the superpowers. Now, Greenland has the political clout to influence Danish security policy, but it also has its own interest in keeping up good relations to the USA especially, because infrastructure and communication are generally dependent on the American presence. The pragmatic policy has been not to challenge the Americans. The ideological policy would have been to stand firm on legal rights.

Notes

1. Jensen, 1977: 70.
2. *Ibid*: 74.
3. *Betænkning* 837/1978: I/ 12f.
4. *Ibid*: 15.
5. Law no. 56, dated 29.11.1978.
6. Lynge, 1988: 16.
7. Lynge, 1981: 13.
8. Grønland 1983: 122.
9. *Grønlands Landstings Forhandlinger*, point 5: "Redegørelse om forløbet af forhandlingerne med De europæiske Fællesskaber", summer 1984: 9f.
10. Rasmussen 1985.
11. *Ibid*.
12. Dahl 1986: 164f.
13. *Ibid*: 205.
14. *Ibid*: 84.
15. *Information* 1984.

16. Lund 1983: 9f.
17. Lidegaard 1983: 101
18. *Folketingets Forhandlinger*, F 13, Feb. 10, 1983, col. 5894f.
19. *Grønlands Landstings Forhandlinger*, point 13: "Redegørelse vedrørende forsvarsområderne i Grønland", autumn 1983. 301 Inuit Circumpolar Conference: Resolutions 77-11; 83-01.
20. *Ibid*.
21. Atuagagdliutit 1984: 34.
22. Brøsted 1985 a + b. and 1987.
23. Brøsted 1985 b and 1987: 7f.
24. Fægteborg 1986: 34.
25. Nielsen 1985 and 1986.
26. Fægteborg 1986: 35.
27. *Ibid*: 35f.
28. *Ibid*: 37.
29. *Ibid*.
30. Redegørelse til Landstinget vedrørende Grønlands forhold til USA. EM 12/1986. Nuuk 16.10.1986.
31. *Politiken* 1987.
32. Dragsdahl 1987 b.
33. Dragsdahl 1987 a.
34. *Folketingets Forhandlinger*, F 14. 9.12.1987, col. 3546
35. *Kristligt Dagblad* 1988.
36. Holstein 1988.
37. *Sermitsiaq* 1989.
38. Rasmussen 1990.
39. Fisker 1988.
40. *Information* 1987.

References

Atuagagdliutit/Grønlandsposten 1984. "Atomvåbcnfrit Grønland". Nuuk. 28.11.1984. Betænkning 837/1978: I: Hjemmestyreordningen.

Brøsted, Jens and Mads Fægteborg 1985a. "An Expulsion of the Great People. When U.S. Air Force Came to Thule. An Analysis of Colonial Myth and Actual Incidents." In: **Jens Brøsted, et.al.** (eds.) 1985: *Native Power*. Universitetsforlaget Bergen, Olso, Stavanger, Tromsø. pp. 213-238.

Brøsted, Jens and Mads Fægteborg 1985b. *Thule – fangerfolk og militæranlæg*. Jurist- og økonomforbundets Forlag. Copenhagen.

Brøsted, Jens and Mads Fægteborg 1987. *Thule – fangerfolk og militæranlæg*. Akademisk Forlag. Copenhagen.

Dahl, Jens 1986. *Arktisk Selvstyre*. Akademisk Forlag. Copenhagen.

Dragsdahl, Jørgen 1987a. "Klart nej fra Siumut til Amerikansk militær legeplads i Grønland". *Information*. Copenhagen. 6.2.1987.

Dragsdahl, Jørgen 1987b. "Thule-radar sprænger Grønlands regering". *Information*. Copenhagen. 23.2.1987.

Fisker, Henrik 1988. "Grønland boykotter færøsk fiskeri i 1989". *Information*. Copenhagen. 28.11.1988.

Fægteborg, Mads 1986. *Thule-sagen. En rapport udarbejdet til Avanersuup Kommunia*. Qaanaaq. February 1986.

Grønland 1983. Yearbook compiled by the Ministry for Greenland. Copenhagen. 1984.

Holstein, Erik 1988. "Låg på strid om base. Opgør om ny NATO-landingsbane på Grønland udskydes". *Det fri Aktuelt*. 10.11.1988.

Information 1984. "Nyt valg i Grønland efter godkendelse af EF-aftale". Copenhagen. 13.3.1984.

Jensen, Einar Lund 1976. *Grønland og EF. En undersøgelse af EF-debatten og dens sammenhæng med den grønlandske debat om hjemmestyre frem til februar 1976*. Kragestedet, Copenhagen.

Kristeligt Dagblad 1988. "USA skal ud". 5.5.1988.

Lidegaard, Bo 1983. "En samtale om ansvar. Interview med Finn Lynge". In: **Poul Claesson** (ed.). 1983: *Grønland Middelhavets Perle. Et indblik i amerikansk atomkrigsforberedelse*. Eirene, Copenhagen. pp. 101-104.

Lund, Henrik 1983. "Forord". In: **Poul Claesson** (ed.). 1983: *Grønland Middelhavets Perle. Et indblik i amerikansk atomkrigsforberedelse*. Eirene, Copenhagen. pp. 9-10.

Lynge, Finn 1981. "Vi vil ikke fjernstyres fra Bruxelles". In: **Bente Hjorth Christiansen** (ed.). 1981: *Grønland på vej*. Folkebevægelsen mod EF. pp. 13-17.

Lynge, Finn 1988. "Conflict treatment, old and new. From Singajuk to EEc and Greenpeace". *Folk*. vol. 30: 5-22. Copenhagen.

Nielsen, Lars Nordskov 1985. "Thule-eskimoernes tvangsflytning". *Politiken*. 13.9.1985.

Nielsen, Lars Nordskov 1986. Thule Inughuit Moved by Force. *IW-GIA Newsletter*. no. 45: 73-85. Copenhagen.

Politiken 1988. "Grønlandsk folketingsmedlem i klemme". Copenhagen. 16.3.1988.

Rasmussen, Lars Toft 1985. "Grønland blev betalt for både fiskene og sikkerheden". *Jydske Tidende*. Koldning. 31.1.1985.

Rasmussen, Søren 1990. "USA indfører brugerbetaling i Søndre Strømfjord. Grønlandsfly skal formentlig betale for at lande på USA's base i Søndre Strømfjord". *Land og Folk*. Copenhagen. 7.3.1990.

Sermitsiaq 1989. "Lukker USA den ene base så lukker Grønland den anden". Nuuk. 2.6.1989.

Memoryscape:

A sense of locality in Northwest Greenland

Mark Nuttall

ABSTRACT
The emergence of a political identity in Greenland since Home Rule should not be taken as something that indicates a culturally homogeneous society. Of importance are differing local identities defined from individual experience and a sense of belonging to a particular community or locality. This article explores a sense of locality in Kangersuatsiaq, a village in the Upernavik district in northwest Greenland. The locality is seen as a *memoryscape*, revealed through stories, memories of specific events, and through place names which tell of subsistence activity and numerous close social associations with the natural environment.

Introduction

When Home Rule was introduced in Greenland in 1979, it was regarded as the outcome of an ethnic conflict between Greenlandic Inuit and Danes, a conflict that stemmed from the impact of Danish colonial and post-colonial policy. During the 1980s, however, there was a gradual shift from an initial Inuit ethnic identity to an identity now defined in political terms (Dahl 1989). The Greenlandic Home Rule government (consisting of native Greenlanders) now claims to represent the interests of both Inuit and Danes living in the country. The transition to political identity is illustrated by Home Rule government aims and policies, which are concerned with increasing revenue from renewable and non-renewable resource exploitation as a way of achieving complete political and economic independence from Denmark. However, while there is a Greenlandic sense of identity *(kalaaliussuseq)*, throughout Greenland there is also diversity in language, history and mode of production, ranging from industrial fishing to seal hunting and sheep breeding. The emphasis on a national Greenlandic identity now comes into conflict with emerging local level identities and interests. Local identity can be said to mediate national identity, but by emphasising nationalism and ignoring locality, the heterogeneous nature of contemporary Greenlandic society is glossed over.

This article discusses the importance of a sense of locality for the inhabitants of Kangersuatsiaq, a village in the southern part of Upernavik district, in northwest Greenland[1]. In Kangersuatsiaq, the way people think and talk about landscape and the physical environment reveals a complex and rich repository of local knowledge used in the cultural construction of community. By focusing on landscape and the area commonly held to be the 'hunting place' *(piniarfik)*, this article outlines notions of locality and community boundary. As will become clear, the locality is a memoryscape, a cultural landscape revealed through its place names, names which are not merely descriptive but tell of subsistence activity and inform us of a multitude of other close human associations with the natural environment (e.g. see Kleivan 1986).

Kangersuatsiaq

Kangersuatsiaq, which has a resident population of some 200, lies to the south of Upernavik town. The name of the village is made up of a root *(kangeq)* ('promontory'/'headland') and the postbase + *(r)suatsiaq*, meaning 'especially big'. The village is more commonly known throughout Greenland by its Danish name, Prøven, meaning 'tried'. Throughout the 1770s attempts were made to establish the successful netting of beluga as an economic activity at the site of present day Kangersuatsiaq. But it was not until 1800 that an approved experiment was set up (Gad 1982: 256), and it is from this date that the history of Kangersuatsiaq is said to start. While whaling was carried out during the nineteenth century, the Inuit population have subsisted mainly by the harvesting of seals. In recent years a smallscale inshore halibut fishery has developed, although the cultural fabric of Kangersuatsiaq remains founded upon and bound up with sealing (Nuttall, in press).

The role of landscape in culture: Some general remarks

In Kangersuatsiaq, as in all areas of the world where landscape plays an important role in culture, the conceptual ordering of experience derives from encounters and interactions with the physical environment. Social anthropologists have shown how northern hunting peoples are inextricably linked with the natural environment both socially and psychologically (e.g. Nelson 1983). This is also a noted feature of hunting and gathering societies worldwide (e.g. for the Australian Aborigines, see Baglin and Moore 1970). Such intimacy is often of a spiritual nature, which has led some writers to see the absence of this in Western consciousness as characteristic of modernity (Carmody 1981). Secular attitudes to landscape are often abhorrent to those peoples for whom the natural environment has deep religious significance (e.g. Toelke 1976). Lopez, writing of human close association with landscape, sees it as an 'archaic affinity' that is 'an antidote to the loneliness that in our own culture we associate with individual estrangement and despair' (Lopez 1986: 266). But even when western attitudes towards landscape see it as something other than a commodity in economic terms, there is a difference between perceptions influenced by, for example, the Romantic poets and those who point out the inherent savagery of nature (e.g. Dillard 1974).

Some anthropologists have been concerned with the analysis of landscape as wilderness and how the dichotomy of village and wild places are central features of cosmology (e.g. see Douglas 1963, on the Lele). The structuralist emphasis on *culture* vs. *nature* has also gone some way, in its concern with the externalization of the environment, in showing how landscape stands apart from the warm secure human world. Myth and fairytale often exemplify this in their treatment of nature as enchanted and a place to fear. Recently, landscape has received more attention from those interested in its symbolic significance. Besson (1979) has shown how the institution of family land among Jamaican peasantries has a symbolic, rather than a practical use. Local authorities and those concerned with rural development regard family land as uneconomic and underproductive. Besson argues that this is a negative ethnocentric perspective. Family land tenure is not inefficient, but symbolizes permanence and continuity of kin groups. Cohen (1987) sees such features of a Shetland landscape as place names, crofting land and peat-banks as elements of a cultural past that act as reference points for orientation in the present. They are features of social identity, while the croft "condenses the past through the landscape itself, and through its associations with the natural calendar; with community; with an earlier mode of subsistence and the ideal of self-sufficiency" (Cohen 1987: 109).

For Inuit groups, the landscape has become the focus of identity and political aspiration (e.g. Price-Bennett 1977, Freeman 1976) although, since Home Rule, the latter is no longer the case in Greenland. My concern in this article is with landscape as a *memoryscape*. This will be elaborated upon in other sections. By way of brief definition, memoryscape is constructed with people's mental images of the environment, with particular emphasis on places as *remembered* places. The area utilized by an individual hunter is part of the community hunting area and, by virtue of belonging to the community, the places a hunter frequents are stamped with indelible marks denoting community. These marks are not visible, but are manifest in place names, in memories of hunting and of past events. All give a sense of a bounded locality distinct from the memoryscape of neighbouring communities. To borrow the often used Lévi-Straussian phrase, places are 'good to think with' and nurture a feeling of belonging.

However, it is the sea (*imaq*), in all its forms, which is the primary physical feature affecting life in Kangersuatsiaq. The population of Kangersuatsiaq and the southern part of Upernavik district has been concerned with sea-use, as opposed to land-use. Historically, there has been a small, but significant exploitation of inland valleys where caribou were hunted. There was caribou hunting in Kangeq between 1850-1922 and in J. P. Koch's Land until the mid-1960s. This is based on informants' information and little exists in the literature which mentions use of the land (except Bryder et al 1921: 430-516, Haller 1986: 97). Today there is no caribou hunting because the caribou population has probably disappeared from the hinterland east of Kangersuatsiaq. In North West Greenland, caribou are now found only in the southern part of Svartenhuk. I agree with Haller that the land "cannot be considered a resource base" (ibid: 97), although sledging routes sometimes involve long detours over the land, usually when the fast sea ice is unstable making winter and spring travel dangerous. I would elaborate upon Haller's observation by arguing that, in the southern part of Upernavik, the land was important in the past and still plays an important role in the cognition of Kangersuatsiaq.

The physical environment is important as the place where a hunter secures the means for his family's existence; in Haller's study he uses the term action space (ibid: 43). As will become clear, it is also 'thought space'. Before discussing the idea of landscape as memoryscape, it is necessary to outline how the Kangersuatsiaq area is perceived and most immediately expressed as community territory.

The physical environment: Local perceptions

The physical environment is perceived by the senses and through the interaction of experience, thought and language it is modified, ordered and conceptualized. People in Kangersuatsiaq talk about the sea-scape and the ice-scape in the same way as the land-scape. All three are contoured and the mind, through language, recognizes and expresses shape and form.

Sea-Scape

As Kangersuatsiaq is an island, people's lives are dominated by the sight and sound of water. Apart from the sky, its many moods provide the subject matter for much casual daily comment, always within the context of talk about the weather. Early in the morning, groups of men gather and discuss the weather. It is usually the first topic of conversation and continual observations are made throughout the day. The Greenlandic word for weather is *sila*. This concept will not be considered in much detail here. For the present discussion it is sufficient to say that in its broadest sense it refers to 'that which is outside', 'the air' and 'the weather'. People look to the sea for their very existence. From it come seals (*puissit*), which give themselves up to the hunter to be converted into meat (*neqi*), fish (*aalisakkat*) and other marine creatures. Dependency involves knowing when and where to hunt. When men discuss the weather, they remark upon the subtle changes in the mood of the sky and the corresponding reactions in the sea. Sila 'moves' and Greenlanders say *'uagut naluarput'/* 'we do not know it'. Sila interacts with, and influences the sea and makes it a calm sea (*imarippoq*) or a strong one (*maliallerpoq*), or brings the wind (*anori*) which causes waves (*malit*) and a rising sea (*qaffiavoq*). People come to recognize when a large wave (*maliarsuk*) is about to become a swelling wave (*ingiulik*), thus placing a hunting trip in a difficult position because of a probable storm (*anorersuaq*), or when it will pass, leaving nothing but a ripple (*minittorneq*).

Sila, by bringing the wind and by changing the sky, ensures the seascape is in a constant flux. However, there are permanent and recurring features, such as eddies (*qalaliatut/* 'things which buble and boil under the water'), or places where one can see the land casting shadows on the water (*qoqaat*). Just as *qoqaat* can darken the sea, the water can also reflect light (*qillaaluttoq*) in certain places and in different seasons. The sea then, is not seen as a featureless expanse of 'broad water' (*imartuneq*); its surface (*imap qaa*) contours twist and change. Wind and tide bring icepans (*kassut*), icebergs (*iluliat*) and movement discernible to an observing eye.

Ice-Scape

The Greenlandic language differentiates between sea ice (*siku*) and freshwater ice (*nilak*). Travel on sea ice requires an understanding of its behaviour and movement. New ice (*sikuliaq*) can be unsafe in parts, with dark patches revealing the sea underneath. Knowledge of where to set foot on fast ice is vital for survival. During summer and early autumn the sea is *sikueruppoq/*'ice-free', or 'has no ice'. In early October thin ice (*sikuaq*) forms in the inner fjord and by middle of November the ice (*siku*) has spread out beyond the bays until the sea is frozen over (*sikuvoq*).

Just as the sea-scape is in motion, the sea ice is not immutable. Icebergs locked into the ice can become almost permanent features for several months, but tidal movements can disrupt them. A smooth flat stretch of ice (*manerak*), which is ideal for sledging, may 'become open water' (*imarorpoq*) and is not to be taken for granted. The ice-scape changes and eventually becomes broken (*manillat*) and a floating pack (*sikorsuit*) during late spring, leaving only fast shore ice (*qanngoq*) which is safe to travel along.

Landscape and community boundary

In Greenland, compared with more nomadic northern hunting peoples (e.g. Riches 1982), Inuit society has been characterized by fixed settlements for several centuries (Petersen 1963). This has meant that groups of people have remained in the same areas, instead of traversing larger parts of the country according to season. The regular return of families to the same campsites during spring and summer, and the constant use of particular hunting areas means each community has its own recognized territory. For the people of Kangersuatsiaq, as for the inhabitants of all other Greenlandic settlements, their hunting and fishing grounds lie within the immediate neighbourhood (Haller ibid.).

The literature on Greenlandic Inuit hunting patterns usually emphasizes two conflicting issues (e.g. see Brøsted 1986; Petersen 1963, 1965). These are:

(1) Greenlandic society is characterized by the freedom of the individual, and combined with this is the recognition that noone owns the animals Inuit hunt. Therefore every individual has the right to use the land and to hunt and fish wherever he wants.
(2) The right to exploit hunting territory is regulated by the community, since it is the local community that controls these areas. Membership of the community is a prerequisite for use of its resource areas. Strangers and outsiders can hunt in another community's area providing they are staying there.

In practice, this second aspect provides the foundation for use. The community both controls and allows access to its hunting territory. Indidividuals have rights over certain areas owing to community allocation which recognizes they have exclusive use. Examples here include netting sites for seal, salmon and beluga, campsites and storage sites. I shall now outline how this works in the Kangersuatsiaq area.

Netting sites

Compiled by me from interviews and regular participation in hunting and fishing trips, *map 1* shows the places where hunters have rights to set nets for seal, salmon and beluga whale. Each hunter has his own netting sites which cannot be used by others, except under certain circumstances as will be seen below. Sons usually inherit the right to use such sites from their fathers. Individual netting sites are found only near the mainland or around small islands, since there are no community regulations restricting rights to set nets around icebergs, where individuals have free access.

Campsites and storage sites

Campsites, usually only occupied during late spring, summer and early autumn, are used by families and have quite often been established for several generations. Tents tend to be erected on the same spots, with areas set aside for relatives and other visitors. In the summer of 1987, when I arrived at Josepi's family campsite near Qeqertaq, I was allotted a place where I could pitch my tent. The following year, I retained my rights to the same site. There was nothing particularly significant about the site in the sense of it being a 'good' or 'bad' site, except that the family I was with had prescriptive rights to it.

At certain points in the landscape, hunters maintain storage sites used for equipment or as meat caches. Hunting equipment may be kept close to netting sites, seal meat is stored for use as dog food when hunters are away for several days, and extra supplies of benzine are taken out to places near the main summer fishing camps. Some families have even started to build hunting huts as a way of marking out their claim to a particular site.

Conditions of use

Sites are allocated to individuals by the community which recognizes that the users have exclusive rights to tenure. This recognition only lasts as long as the individuals continue to *use* the sites. Once use is discontinued, the rights revert to the community and another hunter is then free to take the site over. When a death occurs, a hunter's son relinquishes the right to an inherited site if he chooses not to use it within a 'reasonable' length of time. As an example, an old hunter discontinued use of a salmon netting site at Avalleq, a small island just next to Kangersuatsiaq. After he surrendered his rights, another man decided to set his net

there. The first hunter complained to me that the new user had stolen his site (*"Karl tillipaa"*). But others insisted the rights had reverted to the community, allowing another hunter to take over exclusive use of the site on the basis of his affiliation to the community.

As long as such sites are used and maintained on a regular basis, no other person can establish a claim. Campsites are usually marked out by tent rings, while netting sites may have particular large stones, placed there by the hunter, which are used in securing the net year after year. In addition, the storage of equipment is also a way of marking prescriptive rights.

Although individuals do have privilege of use, which is transferable on the basis of kinship and descent, ultimately it is the community that decides on tenure and access to the hunting territory. In this way, the geographical area becomes a sociological area, with the community imprinted on the landscape in the form of netting sites, local hunting areas, campsites and hunting huts. In the case of inheritance, the community must acknowledge that the inheritor has also used and maintained the sites during his father's lifetime. I do not have any examples of anybody being disinherited by the community because of failure to have done the above. A son will normally inherit sites immediately after his father's death. However, in theory this may not happen, showing that community can be stronger than blood.

Locality

As this article tries to show, subsistence activities take place in a local area expressed, recognized and shared by those who enjoy a common affiliation to their community. Episodes from the past exemplify the importance of locality. For example, people were often killed if they ventured into the hunting area of another community (e.g. Rink 1866: 214). In contemporary Greenland, such extreme treatment of outsiders have now been reduced to silent complaint and joking. However, strangers are still regarded as people to fear. I shall elaborate on this sense of locality in the following. In particular, the significance of places, names and stories (or memories) show how landscape is constituted in relation to the inhabitants of Kangersuatsiaq.

Talking about maps

I had been involved with Josepi's[2] family for some three and a half months when I asked if he could show me, on maps, some of the places where he used to hunt for caribou. My growing confidence in the language was the determining factor in deciding to pursue my interest in mapping areas of the past utilization of land and sea by the older hunters in the village. All the other hunters agreed that if anyone knew anything about the old days (*itsaq*) it would be Josepi.

He immediately showed enthusiasm at my request

and said we could start the following day. It was the end of October and the days were getting shorter. Darkness was beginning to confine Josepi to the village and he now used his time making seal nets in preparation for the winter season. When I arrived, carrying my 1:250 000 scale maps of Kangersuatsiaq and the southern part of Upernavik district, I found Josepi had his own maps ready. He said he was glad I had brought maps which covered such a wide area, as his hunting routes extended from J. P. Koch's Land in the north, to the southern part of Svartenhuk, bordering Uummannaq district, a distance of some 120 km.

I handed the maps to Josepi who, unfolding them, sat forward and sank into silence. I occupied myself with studying the topographic details on Josepi's maps, while he seemed lost in the contours of the land and the myriad of fjords before him. Finally, he put down the map, rolled himself a cigarette, and poured a cup of coffee from the flask he kept under his small table. I went into the kitchen and, taking a mug from the cupboard, helped myself to coffee from the large flask reserved for the rest of the family.

Immediately, Josepi's enthusiasm was infectuous as he then talked at length of the places he would hunt for caribou, first with his father and later with David, his older son. His reminiscences went back as far as 1932 when he first joined his father at the age of nine on a journey to J. P. Koch's Land. Such journeys, undertaken by kayak and umiak (skin boat), would take an average of twenty-two days, he told me. I watched as he traced his numerous expeditions with his finger, weaving in and out of fjords, pointing to places he would stop en route to eat, to hunt, to rest and to camp. He showed me the mountains he wandered among and the rivers he crossed. He told me to mark the places where he had hunted caribou and I noted the dates and the campsites. I felt I was gaining access to a past which contained a different view from contemporary attitudes and responses to the land, particularly those held by younger hunters.

After some two hours of conversation, we were disturbed by Josepi's grandchildren coming home from school. His attention was drawn to other things, to talk of the arrival of the supply boat and of activity down on the pier. I folded my map and went down to watch.

The following day I visited Josepi again. Being so closely associated with his family, hardly a day went by without my spending some time in his house. He asked me if I had brought my map. I said I would go and fetch it, expecting to be told of more hunting expeditions and campsites. Once more, Josepi took the map and spread it on his table. Pointing to part of a small ice-cap close to the inland ice, he said: "This map is wrong. There is no ice here, these are two icecaps, not one." I marked off the part of the map which showed ice. "This, here, is land and there is no ice", Josepi reaffirmed.

Josepi paused, poured himself some coffee, and then returned to the map. Pointing to a spot just to the west of the smallest of the two ice-caps, he told me he had seen a woman's grave there, first in the 1940s and then on later trips. He said her name was Gertuluk and that it was written on a wooden cross. He knew no more about her. But he did remember that the grave was surrounded by wild flowers and that berries grew in abundance. He had first seen it after walking east from Ujarqat Qaqortut ('the white rocks') towards the inland ice, when once in search of caribou. He told me that he could remember that the area was beautiful (alianaak) but that he found no trace of caribou.

Josepi spoke with authority, rolling a cigarette when he seemed satisfied that he could remember no more about Gertuluk. He had told me the cartographers were wrong, his comments made with the confidence of knowing the land, of having traversed it in search of meat. I accepted his version of the map because it had come from his memory. I wondered later whether he had simply been looking at my map in comparison, to check the finer details of his mental map.

An individual hunter's image of the environment evolves in relation to his experience of it. The landscape becomes something which is constituted in relation to each individual. Memory is singularly important because individual ideas are personal and through knowledge and memory hunters 'negotiate images and understandings of the land' (Basso 1984: 22).

Josepi enjoyed reading maps. It was like looking back over a lifetime, with each experience and every hunting trip made familiar. But maps, as Josepi showed me, are profoundly inaccurate in comparison with a hunter's memory of the places they chart. Most older hunters I interviewed had difficulty relating to sheet maps. Place names are often wrong and informants tend to understand oblique aerial photographs far better (see also H. C. Petersen 1986). I found that sheet maps were useful as a reference to which a hunter could 'add his own layers of detailed information' (Brody 1983: 47).

Josepi said he would like to teach me the place names of the surrounding area, the names which could not be found on the map, but that we could start another day. Talking to him started me thinking about the land in another way. It did not seem enough to record land use sites, there were additional layers of meaning to understand.

Later, I studied my maps in the house of Juuna, Josepi's youngest son, marking in his father's routes. I began a conversation with Juuna and he showed me some of the places he had travelled to with Josepi. Pointing to a place, Juuna would say it was 'dark' (taaq), or 'frightening' (ersinaq) or 'beautiful' (alianaak). He showed me the route of a journey he once made to Umiiarfik (a fjord in the Svartenhuk area)

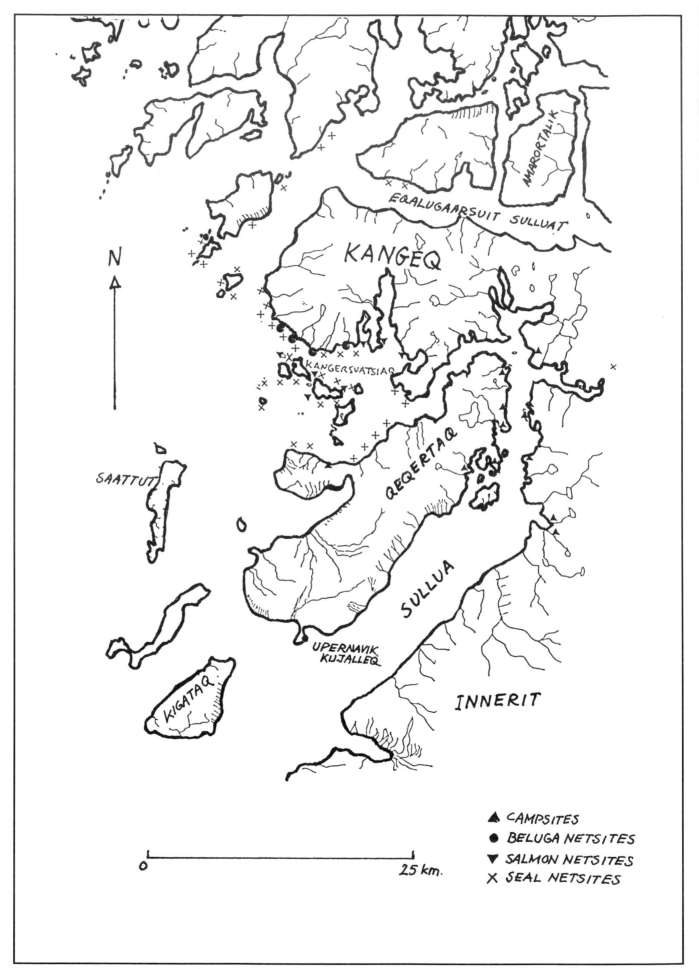

Fig. 1. Netting sites

and I asked him if it was beautiful there. Juuna replied that it was an 'evil' *(ajortoq)* place because he had dreamt of ghosts and strange people living under the earth while camped there.

This led me to attempt to elucidate patterns of thought focused on landscape. What is of interest is how these thought patterns reveal a hidden landscape. The way individuals are predisposed to regard and think about their environment can only be seen with reference to the variables of memory, personality and emotions. I have already sketched out how the environment is immediately perceived by the senses, in terms of knowledge and experience underlying and informing this perception. I now want to build on this a little by considering the above mentioned subjective variables. A useful starting point is to examine place names.

Naming places

Whenever I travelled with Inuit, either in the immediate vicinity of Kangersuatsiaq or on extended trips thoughout the district, I would always mark our routes on 1:250 000 scale maps produced by the Danish Geodetic Institute. To start with, I also found these maps useful for learning about local place names and geographical features. As I have shown though, local knowledge and Danish maps do not always share similar features, especially when different experiences of distances are taken into account. Also, as mentioned above, I began to use local perceptions of landscape as material to fill in the blanks on the 'official maps' and to correct what were seen as mistakes. In addition, careful study of both local land and sea use and the Danish maps reveals three perceptual layers that have been imposed on landscape and environment in Upernavik district. These are the perceptions of colonists and explorers, whalers, and the indigeneous Inuit.

These three perceptual layers manifest themselves in place names and it is their study, known as *onomastics,* that provide a framework within which to work. Onomastics require both an interpretation of place names and a consideration of how close they conform to geography (Robinson 1973). In addition, their etymology involves a discovery of analogy, description and hidden meaning, revealed in memory and in storytelling.

The colonial habit of place naming reduces the landscape to an impersonal piece of territory, previously thought to be devoid of life. For the explorers and colonists, the land was there awaiting 'discovery' and to be claimed for the country they represented. The landscape was seen as empty and claiming by naming 'differed little from dogs pissing on street corners in strange neighbourhoods' (Cooke 1981: 58).

In Upernavik district examples include J. P. Koch's Land, Holm Island, J. A. D. Jensen Islands, and Sanderson's Hope. These are names of explorers, prominent figures and sponsors. Sanderson's Hope at 72° 46'N was named by the Elizabethan explorer John Davis after William Sanderson, one of the sponsors of his 1587 expedition to discover the Northwest Passage. He is said to have named it Sanderson's Hope for the Passage (Lopez 1986: 330). It is a 1042 m high mountain just to the south of Upernavik town and in Greenlandic it is called 'big rock'.

Throughout northern Greenland there are places named after kings, queens, explorers and even societies (e.g. Geographical Society Island at 73° N on the northeast coast). Names can be seen as being possessive in that they indicate ownership by a person or group (Laursen 1972). More importantly, they establish power and territorial claim and historically they tell how 'men of action created names for themselves as they lived' (Robinson 1973: 323). As for the practice of naming places after royalty, one polar explorer, exemplifying the attitude of the exploring fraternity, suggests that critics "...should ask themselves whom else but royalty they would choose if they set out to do honour to the highest in their land" (Debenham 1942: 544).

Throughout the eighteenth and nineteenth centuries, Scottish and English whalers systematically exploited the waters in Upernavik district and are responsible for several place names, such as Sugar Loaf, Dark Head and Horse Head. The whalers, as indeed the explorers, took their own cognitive stereotypes with them into the Arctic. Their expectations were informed by those who went before them and the Arctic was seen as an unforgiving wilderness. Much of this was expressed in song and ballad:

> *Now Greenland is a horrid place*
> *Where our fisher lads have to go*
> *Where the rose and the lily never*
> *bloom in spring*
> *And there's only ice and snow*
> *   ('The Greenland Whale Fishery',*
> *   nineteenth century traditional*
> *   whaling song.)*

Successive waves of whalers, explorers and travellers ventured into the Arctic and specific images emerged based on their accounts. Subjective impressions were allowed to colour published journals of whaling voyages and of exploration and this led to an image others internalized and upon which they based their own ideas. Writing was influenced by immediate impressions and by the author's situation, such as the hardships endured, cold, inadequate equipment, homesickness, starvation and the death of fellow crew members. Image and geographical reality occasionally overlapped when it came to place naming, for example Devil's Thumb in the north of Upernavik district.

All this points to the importance of memory, personality and emotion as variables in the perception of

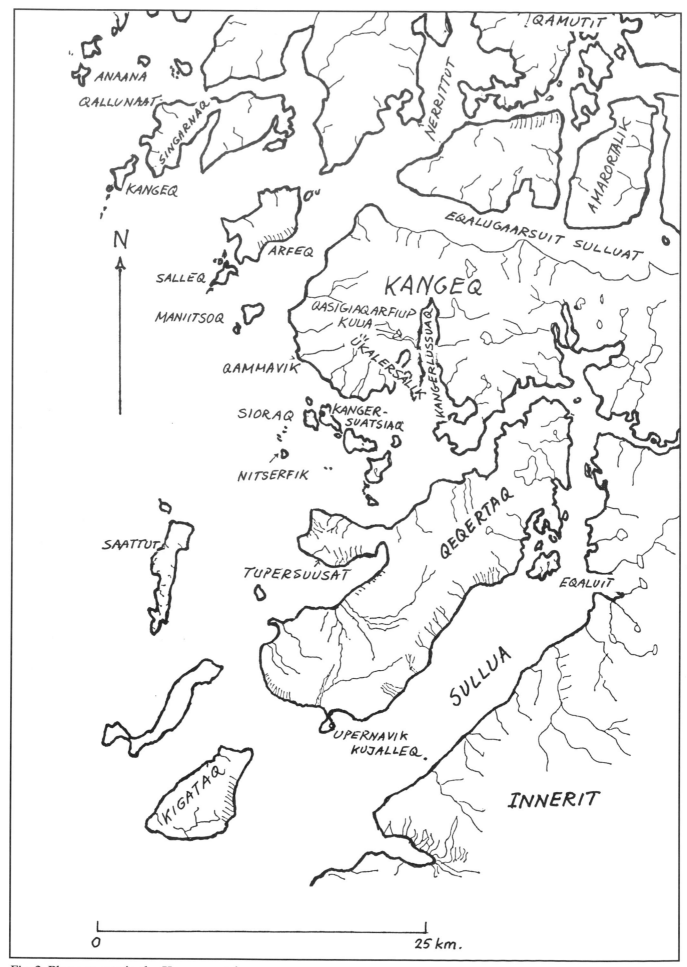

Fig. 2. Place names in the Kangersuatsiaq area

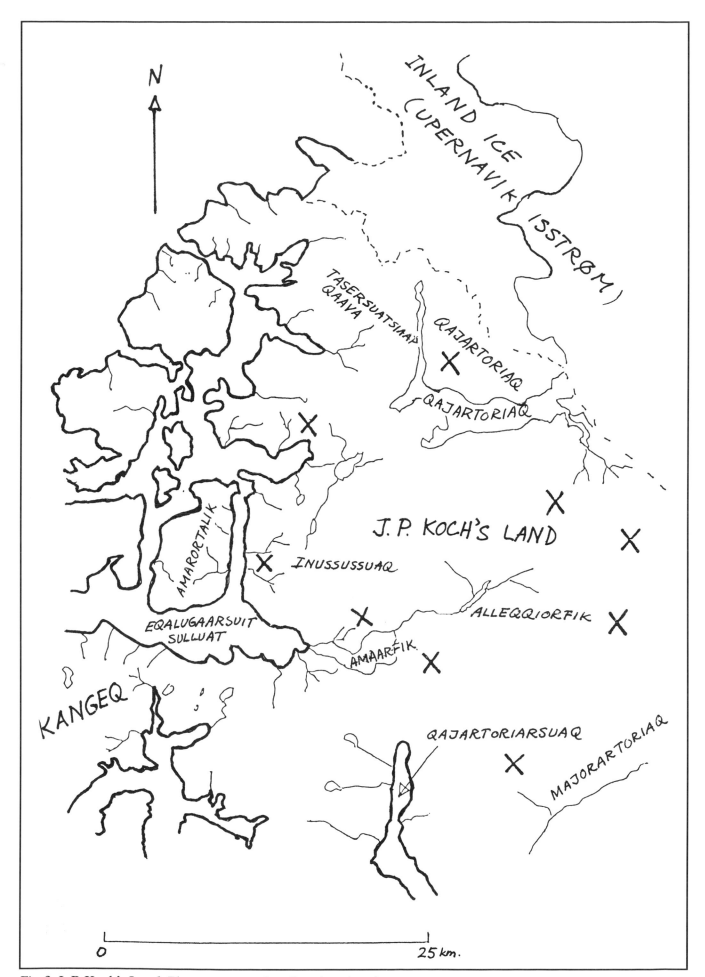

Fig. 3. J. P. Koch's Land. Place names and caribou hunting sites.

landscape and the environment. For the purpose of this discussion I am interested in how these variables inform us of the Inuit relationship with the environment and it is which this I now turn.

Memoryscape

Greenlandic place names in the Kangersuatsiaq area and in the rest of Upernavik district differ from the Danish names given to the same localities. This also holds for the rest of Greenland (Petersen 1985). Greenlandic names do not necessarily conform to geography, but they are multidimensional. This means they contain a physical, mythical, factual and historical meaning (see also Robinson 1973).

Each of these meanings overlap and converge. There are places which refer specifically to physical features such as Kangeq ('headland'), Kangersuatsiaq ('little headland'), Sioraq ('sand island'). Qeqertaq ('island'), Kangerlussuaq ('big fjord'), Singarnaq ('yellowish grey'), Ikerasaq ('sound' or 'channel'), Saatoq('thin, flat stone island') and Majuariaq ('hill').

Other names reflect analogy. Such places require a more powerful toponymical designation because they serve to remind people of other realms of experience and culture which transcends geography. Examples in the Kangersuatsiaq area include Iviangernat ('twin peaks resembling a woman's breasts'), Maniitsoq (an island resembling 'hummocky ice'), Toornaarsutoq ('little spirit'), Salleq ('the island in front of the inhabited place'), Qallunaaq ('Dane') and Anaana ('mother').

The majority of place names inform us of land and sea use, both in the present and in the past. Fig. 2 reveals a landscape named not because of features immediately apparent, but due to the importance of these places in subsistence activities, human activity and fellowship. The places I have marked on the map include:

Qammavik – this sea cave means 'a place where hunters lie in wait for sea mammals'.
Ukalersalik – 'a place where one finds Arctic hare'(ukaleq).
Arfeq – 'walrus'.
Qasigiarfiup Kuua – 'river which belongs to the place of the spotted seal'.
Eqaluit – pl. of eqaluk meaning 'Arctic char'.
Qamutit – 'sled'.
Tupersuusat – 'a camping place'.
Nerrittut – 'the eaters', i.e. a place where 'they eat together'.

Fig. 3. shows past caribou hunting areas in J. P. Koch's Land. Again, the Greenlandic place names illustrate the utilization of the landscape, particularly summer and autumn activities:

Amaarfik – 'a place from where the kayaks are carried up'.
Qajartoriaq – 'a lake (or other place) where kayaks are used'.
Majorartoriaq – 'a river where one can climb up' (with a boat or a kayak).
Allerqiorfik – 'a place of the long-tailed duck'.
Inussussuaq – 'big cairn'.

An interesting comparison with the explorers is that in Greenland Inuit seldom, if ever, name places after people. Petersen notes an exception in Maniitsoq district where there is a place called Kamillakkut (meaning 'the Kamilla family'), which was probably a kin based summer campsite (Petersen 1963: 276).

But whatever place names say about geography, analogy or subsistence activities, many have an additional layer of meaning. It is precisely that which is hidden and invisible in the land which is often neglected. Stories and myths unfold against a geographical backdrop. Events, whether contemporary, historical or mythical, that happen at certain points in the local area tend to become integral elements of those places. They are thought about and remembered with reference to specific events and experiences and it is in this sense I refer to landscape as memoryscape. Memories take the form of stories about real and remembered things. They cannot be separated from the land even though place names do not immediately reflect such stories. Some place names may be mnemonic devices, triggering a collective memory of an event that has significance for the community:

In the old days, when people lived on Maniitsoq (a small island north of Kangersuatsiaq, MN), they would sometimes travel to Kangersuatsiaq. There came a time when people were frightened to do this because of a powerful angakkoq who lived at Qammavik. At first, some hunters did not return home to Maniitsoq in their kayaks. It was thought they had capsized at Kinnguvik ('the place where one capsizes'). Then more hunters disappeared, until one returned to tell of the angakkoq. The angakkoq was evil and jealous of other hunters. He would lie in wait in his kayak at Qammavik until a hunter passed by with a seal. He would paddle his kayak behind the hunter until he was close enough to kill him and steal his seal. Some say the hunters went together and killed the angakkoq, but others say he saw them coming and flew away from Qammavik in his kayak over Kangeq to the mountains. (Transscript of several versions of a story told about Qammavik).

Other places contain within them stories that have a more individual memory about isolated events:

I will tell a story about Arfeq. I remember a man who once made a beautiful harpoon head. The first time he went out hunting with it he spotted a walrus on an ice floe. He paddled his kayak very carefully until he was close enough to throw his harpoon. He took aim and threw it, but the walrus dived. Pulling in his harpoon, he noticed the harpoon head had disappeared, but the shaft and the bladder float were still there. he looked around but could not see the walrus.

Feeling depressed at the disappearance of the walrus and the loss of the harpoon head he returned home. Later, during the evening, he went to visit his friend who was a big hunter. Still in low spirits, he told his friend of the day's event and of the loss of the beautiful harpoon head. However, his friend laughed and, reaching into his pocket, he said: 'Today I was out in my kayak and you thought I was the walrus! Here is your harpoon head!

When I was a child I used to hear a story about Aappilattoq. It was dark and a ship was sailing towards the village. The children were very afraid because they thought some Qallunaat (Danes or Europeans, MN) were coming to make war with the Inuit. They began screaming and crying and nobody could calm them. An old woman, who was a sorceress (ilisiitsoq), told the people to put out all the lights. She then went down to the water's edge and let down her hair. She dipped her hair in the water and told the ship to go away, because it was making the children afraid. She pulled her hair out of the water and the lights in the ship went out. The people saw that now instead of the ship there was an iceberg. Sometimes I think of the things that happened in my country, in the past.
(Both stories told by Matheus L., aged 78).

Place names are important in story telling because they are "situating devices, as conventionalized instruments for locating narrated events in the physical settings where the events have occurred" (Basso 1984: 32). Such individual recollection becomes part of the community repertoire and gives access to a past that provides a direct link to the present. Taken from my field notes, the story that follows is a version of four corresponding accounts told to me by the actors involved:

In January 1986, two of Eirik's dogs disappeared from the village. They had been chained up outside Josepi's house and nobody in the village had seen them escape. Several days later, Eirik, Josepi and David set off to set their nets in the Salleq area. They planned to spend the night in the hunter's hut on the island where they would be joined by Peter and Abeli, two brothers from Kangersuatsiaq. All five men arrived at Salleq together and were the first hunters to use the hut that winter. Climbing up to the hut, they noticed footprints in the snow leading towards the hut and another set leading away into the mountains. On entering, the men found Eirik's two dogs lying dead on the floor. Along the window sills several candles had burned the length of their wicks, leaving pools of hard, melted wax.

For the purpose of this discussion, I am not concerned with an interpretation of such stories, but rather to show how places become remembered places. This particular story points to something that is feared in the landscape. But it does illustrate how a place such as Salleq becomes known as 'the place where Eirik's dogs were found dead', just as other places are ingrained in individual and collective memory as 'where I killed a walrus last autumn', or 'my father used to have seal nets over there'. For example, in August 1988, Josepi took Juuna to J. P. Koch's Land, a place he had last visited in 1966. On this latest trip, the two men had hoped to find caribou. They were unsuccessful and found nothing except Josepi's footprints at the site of his last camp.

Because hunting activity is 'carried out within certain de facto environmental boundaries' (Haller 1986: 146), knowledge does not usually extend to other community hunting areas. A change in place names indicating differences in dialect, or suffixed with -kassak ('bad' i.e. 'of no significance for hunting') usually denotes a boundary at which subsistence activity stops. Within their own area, hunters have no difficulty finding their way about, quite often in bad weather and fog. On several occasions I travelled with people in areas other than Kangersuatsiaq. Unfamiliarity with places, sudden storms and white-outs sometimes resulted in us getting lost. An area such as Melville Bay, for example, is a memory-desert where 'each little place with its name and legend produced a vivid pause in the imagination' (Gunn 1969: 34). An area, while familiar to those who hunt and live there, nonetheless becomes unknown territory to those who have no knowledge or memory of it. Memory is a way of articulating the relationship between community and landscape, or between the landscape and an individual. Traces of memory are left in the immediate area, ensuring the writing of subsistence and other activities on the landscape.

Geography is extended to include an 'existentialist realm' (Tuan 1971: 183) and necessitates a consideration of *meaning*. In the Kangersuatsiaq area, the organization of geographical space involves a contemplative process whereby experience and memory are important considerations when trying to understand the locality. There is a fusion of spatial and cognitive symmetry. The environment is perceived in a particular way and people are involved in a dialogue with a landscape suffused with memory and highly charged with human energy.

Tuan sees the ordering of space as the result of 'man's need to discern order' (ibid: 184). Building on this, I consider what I have termed memoryscape as illustrating how the landscape is modified and culturally constructed. Through land and sea use, myth and historical events, an image of the community is reflected in the landscape. The community boundaries are extended into abstract space which then becomes an integral part of the community. Places in this area resonate with community consciousness. Such places are *reference* points, or what Robinson calls *archives* when he talks about 'the elusive identity hidden in the archives of the named cultural items, as well as people, that distinguish the landscape' (1973: 333).

In a contemporary hunting community such as Kangersuatsiaq, a hunter who daily criss-crosses the local area is aware of and involved with land, sea and ice. Each hunter has his own indelible personal memories, his own version of Josepi's footprints, as it were. His relationship with the environment is informed by these memories, for 'without memory or the sense of historic continuity the man-land relationship remains overly economic; without economic control the relationship remains only spatial' (Burghardt 1973: 244).

There are stories, place names and individual experiences far too numerous to record. But every such event contributes to the creation of a landscape which is alive with recollection. For the people of Kangersuatsiaq, their local environment is a living place. Some areas may be good hunting territory, or notable char runs, or places to fear, or the scene of some great personal adventure. A picture emerges of a totality, a landscape that belongs to the community precisely because it is continually constructed during a continuous process of modification. The landscape and local environment is revealed in contours on the cognitive map used by individuals to orientate themselves and their sense of community in relation to it. Memories, names, and land and sea use are existential responses to what is originally abstract and unfamiliar. To interpret the Kangersuatsiaq hinterland as a sociological area one must be aware of ideology and personal as well as collective meaning. The Inuit relationship with the landscape involves an affinity that, in a Wordsworthian sense, is 'far more deeply interfused' precisely because it transcends mere economic exploitation of natural resources. The structuralist notion of a culture vs. nature dichotomy is far too simple because both realms overlap. Each encompasses and informs the other.

Conclusion – locality and identity

This article has explored the idea of landscape and the natural environment as a memoryscape. As such, it is the physical expression of Kangersuatsiaq and gives a sense of locality important for social continuity and identity. Subsistence activities take place in a specific environment that forms part of a larger system of memory, thought and existence. The landscape is rich in human close association, "invested with significance in personal or family history" (Nelson 1983: 243). Recognition of this can increase our understanding of modern Greenland and inform debates about identity. While the local landscape is an expression of community, the emphasis on a national Greenlandic identity obviates recognition of this. The study of localities, together with an understanding of the meaning of place names and local perceptions of the environment, illustrates the rich cultural fabric of modern Greenland.

Notes

1. Fieldwork was carried out for twenty months in 1987-88 and funded by the Economic and Social Research Council. For a fuller ethnography of Kangersuatsiaq see Nuttall (1990).
2. Josepi is a pseudonym for the head of the family with whom I lived during my residence in Kangersuatsiaq. I have chosen to protect the anonymity of people who may not wish to see their name in print.

References

Baglin, D. and D. Moore 1970. *People of the Dreamtime*. Walker/Weatherhill: New York.

Basso, Keith H. 1984. "Stalking with stories: names, places and moral narratives among the Western Apache". In E. Bruner (ed.), *Text, Play and Story*. Proceedings of the American Ethnological Society, Washington D. C. 1983.

Besson, J. 1979. "Symbolic aspects of land tenure in the Caribbean". In M. Cross & A. Marks (eds.), *Peasants, Plantations and Rural Communities in the Caribbean*. Department of Sociology, University of Surrey.

Brice-Bennet, Carol (ed.) 1977. *Our Footprints are Everywhere*. Labrador Inuit Association: Nain.

Brody, Hugh 1983. *Maps and Dreams*. Penguin: Harmondsworth.

Bryder, H. et al, 1921. "Upernavik Distrikt". In G. C. Amdrup et al (eds.), "Grønland i Tohundredaaret for hans Egedes Landing". *Meddelelser om Grønland 60: 430-516.*

Brøsted, Jens 1986. "Territorial rights in Greenland: some preliminary notes". *Arctic Anthropology 23 (1 & 2) : 325-338.*

Burghardt, A. 1973. "The bases of territorial claims". *Geographical Review 63: 225-245.*

Carmody, D. L. 1981. *The Oldest God: Archaic Religion Yesterday and Today*. Abingdon: Nashville.

Cohen, Anthony P. 1987. *Whalsay: Symbol, Segment and Boundary in a Shetland Island Community*. Manchester University Press: Manchester.

Cooke, A. 1981. "A gift outright: the exploration of the Canadian High Arctic islands after 1800". In M. Zaslow (ed.), *A Century of Canada's Arctic Islands 1880-1980*. Royal Society of Canada: Ottawa.

Dahl, Jens 1989. "From ethnic to political identity". *Nordic Journal of International Law 3: 312-315.*

Debenham, F. 1942. "Place names in polar regions". *Polar Record 3 (24) : 541-542.*

Dillard, A. 1974. *Pilgrim at Tinker Creak*. Harper's Magazine Press: New York.

Douglas, Mary 1963. *The Lele of Kasai*. Oxford University Press: Oxford.

Freeman, Milton (ed.) 1976. *Inuit Land Use and Occupancy Project, Vol. 1-3*. Department of Indian and Northern Affairs: Ottawa.

Gad, Finn 1982. *The History of Greenland, Vol. 3*. Nyt Nordisk Forlag: København.

Gunn, N. 1969. *The Silver Darlings*. Faber and faber: London.

Haller, A. 1986. *The Spatial Organization of the Marine Hunting Culture in the Upernavik District, Greenland*. Universitetet Bamberg: Bamberg.

Kleivan, Inge 1986. "De grønlandske stednavnes vidnesbyrd om vandringer og forskellige aktiviteter". In *Vort sprog – vor kultur*. Proceedings of a symposium held in Nuuk, October 1981. Ilisimatusarfik and Kalaallit Nunaata Katersugaasivia. Pilersuiffik: Nuuk.

Laursen, D. 1972. "The place names of Greenland". *Meddelelser om Grønland 180 (2).*

Lopez, B. 1986. *Arctic Dreams*. Macmillan: London.

Nelson, R. K. 1983. *Make Prayers to the Raven*. Chicago University Press: Chicago.

Nuttall, Mark 1990. *Names, Kin and Community in Northwest Greenland.*. Ph. D. dissertation, University of Cambridge.

Nuttall, Mark in press. "Sharing and the ideology of subsistence in a Greenlandic sealing community". *Polar Record.*

Petersen, H. C. 1986. "Recording the utilization of land and sea resources in Greenland". *Arctic Anthropology 23 (1 & 2): 259-270.*

Petersen, Robert 1963. "Family ownership and right of disposition in Sukkertoppen district, West Greenland". *FOLK 5: 269-281.*

Petersen, Robert 1965. "Some regulative factors in the hunting life of Greenlanders". *Folk 7: 107-124.*

Petersen, Robert 1985. "Danske stednavne i Grønland". In B. Jørgensen (ed.), *Stednavne i brug: Festskrift udgivet i anledning af Stednavneudvalgets 75 års jubilæum*. C. A. Reitzels Forlag: København.

Riches, David 1982. *Northern Nomadic Hunter Gatherers: A Humanistic Approach*. Academic Press: London.

Rink, Heinrich J. 1866. *Eskimoiske Eventyr og Sagn*. C. A. Reitzels Boghandel: København.

Robinson, B. S. 1973. "Elizabethan society and its named places". *Geographical Review 63: 322-333.*

Toelke, B. 1976. "Seeing with a native eye: how many sheep will it hold?" In W. Capps (ed.), *Seeing with a Native Eye*. Harper: New York.

Tuan, Y. F. 1971. "Geography, phenomenology and the study of human nature". *Canadian Geographer 15 (3): 181-192.*

Definitions of Nation

in European political thought

Uffe Østergård

ABSTRACT

"Nation" is a concept of which no generally accepted definition exists. This essay traces two conflicting definitions that were important in the 19th century and still influence debates on nationalism.

The objective-cultural definition has its roots in Johann Gottfried Herder's ideas. He saw national differences as the leading principle of historical development. The different nations both had a right and a duty to realize their destiny. Both among reactionaries (e.g. Joseph de Maistre) and radicals (e.g. Giuseppe Mazzini) such an objective definition was accepted during the 19th century. In this understanding people belonged to a nation irrespective of their own will or consciousness.

Since it has been very difficult in practice to agree on which nations had the right to exist, there have been attempts to fall back on a subjective definition of nation. Joseph Ernest Renan argued for such an understanding when after 1870 and the German conquest he tried to explain why the people of Alsace and Lorraine actually had the right to belong to France. While German nationalists argued that the inhabitants were objectively German and should be given back their true identity, Renan claimed that , in spite of their German language and race, they were French because they identified themselves with France. The nation was a political community, and people should belong to it by their own choice.

Attempts to unite the subjective and objective definitions and translate them into practical politics were made by the Austrian socialists Karl Renner and Otto Bauer. They both stressed cultural autonomy for nations, while holding that territorial units should not be based on national allegiance. The Bolsheviks criticized the Austro-Marxists on the grounds of two opposed principles: on the one hand, their limitation of the rights of nations to self-determination; on the other hand, their encouraging of unwished for national feelings.

The conflicting definitions of nation have placed a heavy burden on political thought in the 20th century resulting in vague and conflicting ways of justifying nationality, with which we still have to struggle in the future.

Nation and state

In political theory it has never been possible to agree on how to define state and nation. This deficiency has not really been alleviated by modern historical and sociological reasearch. In everyday language, the nation is the same as the state. States are often called nations, state income accounts are called national products. The UN is an organization of legally defined, sovereign states, where the nation signifies the sum of citizens within the state authority's geographical boundaries. There is nothing really wrong with this, but it does slur the importance of the nationalist ideology, i.e., the conscious construction of a common pre-history that for many people in Europe of the 1800's and in the Third World today has become precisely the legitimisation of the successful state units. The essential point in nationalism's claim to the existence of a common cultural identity in "folk" as the prerequisite of

the state unit is thus easily lost. The "German nation" is often said to be a language fellowship, the Swiss a historical fellowship, the Pakistani a religious fellowship and the American Indian nation a fellowship of shared fate. But how does it fit in with the claim that the nation is the bearer of the state, the claim that is basic to the international legal order within the United Nations – which is composed of states?

Herder and "Volksgeist"

In the late 18th century, the German Enlightenment philosopher Johann Gottfried Herder (1774-1803) conceived of national differences as the guiding principle of world history. He was not a pan-Germanic nationalist and recognised both the right (and duty) of the Slavs and the Scandinavians, the French and the Italians to practice their own national destiny. He was not interested in nationality for its own sake but in the question of cultural differences. This became the basis for the theoretical programme of historicism. But the concept of *Volksgeist* that appeared in his manuscripts from 1774 proved to have wide-spread and fateful consequences. In a way he just continued in the line of Montesqieu's thinking that particular conditions lay at the basis of any people's life and institutions. But Herder radicalized this to the point where any idea about general laws and rules became untenable. No general principle could be separated from its local conditions of origin such as goodness, truth and beauty. Herder and the romantic historicists traced all that back to history, which Enlightenment philosophers had assumed was common and unchangeable in mankind. For Herder it was not history that could be made rational (as did Voltaire (1694-1778)), but rationality that was historical.

Man is subordinate to nation

This originally progressive programme led directly to an anti-revolutionary, cultural, "objective" definition of the nation, for example such as one finds in a pamphlet entitled *Considérations sur la France* from 1814, written by the reactionary French philosopher Joseph de Maistre (1753-1821), who was also the ambassador for the kingdom of Sardinia (Piemonte) in St. Petersburg.

> "Like all its predecessors, the Constitution of 1795 was made for man . But there is no *man* in the world. I have seen Frenchmen, Italians and Russians; thanks to Montesqieu, I know *that one can be a Persian* ; but as far as mankind is concerned, I declare that never in my life have I met one; if they can be found, I am ignorant of them."[1]

This view of history imputes that nation stood against nation, and that these were not created by the will of their members, but on the contrary, that the members' will was dependent on their belonging to the totality of the nation. Man is a product of his circumstances and not vice versa, as the Enlightenment philosophers believed – a theory for which Holberg had already criticised Montesqieu. How can one explain the differences between the Greeks, the Romans and the Israeli on the basis of climate? Instead, Holberg used the differences between the regimes as an explanation of national differences.

Advantages of the principle of cultural nationality

The classic statement of the absolute advantages of the principle of objective cultural nationality was presented by the radical Italian Democrat Giuseppe Mazzini (1805-72) in 1857. On the threshold of the invasion of Sicily, led by Garibaldi in 1859, Mazzini drafted an Utopian division of Europe into "national" units. He prescribed 11 units, *all* of which would in reality be *multinational* – with Italy as the only telling exception, in our way of thinking as well as following the thought of the 19th century:

> "Spain and Portugal united: the Iberian Peninsula. Sweden, Denmark and Norway united: the Scandinavian Peninsula. England, Scotland and Ireland: the United Great Britain. Italy, from the farthest tip of Sicily to the Alps, including Italian Tyrol, Ticino, Corsica, etc.: united as one state. Switzerland with Savoy, German Tyrol, Carinthia and Carniola (part of the present Slovenia) turned into an "Alpine Confederation". "Hellenes" (Greece) with Epirios, Thessaly, Albania, Macedonia, Rumelia up to the Balkan Mountains, including Constantinople. Constantinople ought to be the capital, under Greek rule, in a confederation of races (European and Christian) which today comprise the Turkish Empire – i.e., Eastern Austria – Bosnia, Serbia and Bulgaria (that would make your British explode). Austria ought to disappear: one great Danube-confederation: Hungary, the Romanian race, Walachia, Moldavia, Transylvania, Hercegovina) Bohemia, ect., Germany including the Netherlands and part of Belgium (Flanders) France including the French part of Belgium (Wallon), Russia and Poland: the rest divided between them: two separate nationalities in confederation. All this, my dear, is a book coming generations must write, because I am so involved with the Italian parts in particular that I do not have the time."[2]

Clearly, this was a programme that did not care much for the demands of the various national movements, but simply aimed at creating "viable" states.

With the intentions stated, Mazzini could allow himself such free hands, doing as he liked. Since it was purely a speculative project, no one would attempt to put it into practice. Still the attempt is representative of much that was sought turned into political action by others. Mazzini's theoretical basis was a particular idea of what constitutes a nation. For him, a nation was created out of political loyalties. These were not chosen by chance. The collective unit could only find expression in one, independent nation-state with one language. For Mazzini the nation-state was not a goal in itself – as it was for so many other political theorists – it was the *means* to realise egalitarian democracy. As the world looked then, he could only imagine this democracy surviving in relatively large states. Therefore this programme, which despite its hypothetical character contains many parallels with the programme resulting from the WWI peace negotiations, which was based on the American President Wilson's doctrine of national self-determination. Yet, although the principle of self-determination was exercised in Eastern and Central Europe, all the newly established states, except the losers Austria and Hungary, were in fact multi-national states, even though they called themselves national states. As is well-known, since then this led to the suppression, in the name of "national unity", of large national minority groups.

One nation accepted as such by the people

It has proven impossible to agree on an "objective" definition of nation. Actually, since the French Revolution most wars have been fought over conflicting versions of national and historic "rights". We all fall back on the operational and apparently simple phrasing that any group of people who define themselves as a nation, or are seen by others as being one, are one.

This is how Joseph Ernest Renan (1823-1892), a French expert on the Orient and a student of religions, argued in 1882 in what has since become one of the standard texts among studies of nationalism: *Qu'est-ce qu'une nation?* His object was to "scientifically" demonstrate that the French population in Alsace-Lorraine had the "right" to their own, French, nationality, even after the provinces had been signed over to Germany in 1871. The French had earlier favoured the objective definition of national identity. However, after their defeat in the French-German war, they changed their minds, as did the Danes after their defeat in 1864, followed in 1867 by the incorporation into Prussia of all of Slesvig. Renan asked rhetorically, but quite to the point:

> "But what is a nation then? Why are the Netherlands a nation, when Hannover or the Duchy of Parma is not? How is it that France continues to be a nation, when the principle that created it (the monarchy U.Ø.) has disappeared? Why is Switzerland, with its three languages, two religions and three or four races, one nation, while Tuscany for example, which is so homogeneous, is not? Why is Austria a state and not a nation? And how does the principle of nationality differ from the principle of race?"[3]

Aside from the fact that today, after WWII and Nazism, we do not treat the principle of race lightly, these are both relevant and complicated questions. The occasion of Renan's speculations was that the respected German ancient historian Theodor Mommsen (1817-1903) and the left-Hegelian philosopher David Friedrick Strauss (1808-74) had presented their "scientific" contribution to the German war effort and the creation of a state under Prussian dominance by justifying the conquering of Alsace-Lorraine/Elsass-Lothringen, proclaiming the population part of the German *"Volkgeist"*. They thus joined the long discussion on whether nationality is determined by spirit or determined by contract, which had been going on since Montesqieu, Herder, Voltaire and since the German war of liberation against Napoleon. The German historians justified the occupation by referring to the unconscious forces driving individual beings: language, race and historical tradition. People in Alsace spoke German and were part of German culture, therefore the occupation was legitimate.

French scholars, naturally, responded to this challenge by "proving" the Alsaciens' "right" to remain French. The most convincing answer was given by Renan in the speech quoted above: *Qu'est-ce qu'une nation?* , playing on the famous speech by Abbé Sieyès in 1789: *What is the third estate?* The main difficulty for Renan and the historical sociologist Fustel de Coulange (1830-89) was the fact that up till 1870 they had been proponents of an objective definition of nationality along the same lines as Herder's *Volkgeist* – Fustel de Coulange in his capacity of professor of history at the university in Strasbourg 1861-70. But this principle did not apply in this case , where it was a question of a German speaking population, who sang *"O Tannenbaum"* in German at Christmas and at the same time demanded the right to sing the *"Marseillaise"* in French on July 14. How could this conflict between different definitions be resolved?

The subjective determination of nation: Renan

After thoroughly testing the arguments for and against the various definitions – which is what still makes Renan's text of key importance in the history of the theory of nationalism – he gave up trying to demonstrate the Celtic roots, the socalled "race", of the Alsacien population. On the contrary, he admitted without reservation that the Alsaciens were German by language and race – but despite this, French by disposition. This had not always been the case. In 1789, the boundaries of France were neither logical nor necessary. During the century after the Westphalian Treaty in 1648, the French monarchy had conquered large areas of land in the northeast, which had formerly belonged to the German empire. But the ties between the provinces were the shared relationship to the common dynasty, in the same way as the conquering of Ireland and Scotland by the English royal house only resulted in a dynastic union.

At the end of the 18th century, the nation freed itself of the king and realised the highest ideals of political enlightenment in a new "spiritual union" within the boundaries that had been created by the despised dynasty over 800 years of continous expansion and consolidation of power. In this way, France became a nation without the dynasty that had created the preconditions for it just as USA and Switzerland which had each in their own ways achieved a similar status. After the Revolution the French nation defined itself as a *political* union with the strengths and weaknesses entailed by the element of conscious choice. The majority of the German-speaking inhabitants in the province of Alsace had joined the new revolutionary union during the Revolution in the 1790s (in contrast to the German Rhine provinces, which had been incorporated into France under Napoleon, but never been asked). Renan emphasized in his argument that they did not want to become a part of the German realm, that they felt suppressed and preferred the French political union symbolised by the republican tricouleur, the *Marseillaise* and the figure of Marianne. As he put it at another occasion:

> *"They talk of France's right and Germany's right, but ought to talk of the Alsaciens' right not to obey other authorities than those they have agreed to obey."*[4]

This led to the following famous definition of national allegiance:

> *"A "Zollverein" (the German Customs Union from 1834 to 1866. U.Ø.) is no fatherland (...) A nation is a soul, a spiritual principle (...) A nation is one great sense of solidarity, formed by the experiences with the sacrifices it has made in the past, and those it is willing to make in the future (...) A nation's existence is a daily plebiscite."*[5]

This "subjective" definition of nationality is what remains from the "scientific" debate at the end of the 19th century, stirred by the events of that time. But that is quite a lot in fact. It emphasizes will, solidarity and a feeling of fellowship in the population, whichever way they be determined. And what is most important in this context, it emphasizes the organised political framework within which this subjectivity is expressed – the state.

Subjective nationality as practical politics – The Habsburg Monarchy

The logical consequence of Renan's subjective concept of a nation must be to accept cultural autonomy within the existent states, whether these are nationally defined or not. This, in the case of France, Renan did not. On the contrary, he was an eager supporter of the systematic centralisation and nationalisation of the Third Republic introduced by Jules Ferry's school reform as well as other elements of modernisation so well described by Eugen Weber in his book *"Peasants into Frenchmen"* (1976).

The first serious attempt to turn the subjective definition of nation into practical politics were made around the turn of the century by the Austrian socialists Karl Renner and Otto Bauer in an effort to protect their United Socialist Party during the crisis inflicted upon it by the nationalist opposition, particularly the Czech trades unions. In 1897 the United Socialists had split into six national federations, one German, one Czech, one Polish, one Ruthian, one Italian and one Yougoslavian (south-Slavic). In 1899, a far-reaching if vaguely phrased programme for the internal independence of individual nationalities in the Austrian-Hungarian double monarchy was adopted, the socalled *Brünner Nationalitäten-Programm* (after the Czech town Brno). It called for the transformation of the empire into a confederation with guarantees of cultural autonomy to all minorities. However, the compromise did not stand up. Despite warnings from the Second International convening in Copenhagen in 1910, the Czechs formed their own party in 1911. The joint multi-national trades union had already been dissolved in 1905. During the ensuing discussions, the German Austrians Karl Renner and Otto Bauer fundamentally re-thought the question of nationality, modifying the disjointed, pan-Germanic remarks made by Marx around 1848-49, which had so far constituted Marxist "theory" of the nation.

After 1899, Karl Renner[6] (1870-1950), a lawyer by training, became thoroughly absorbed in studies of the nation question and of the possibilities of a reformation of the Austrian-Hungarian empire. This undertaking of his was facilitated by the victory of the socialists in the 1899-elections, following which Renner found peace of research while working as a librarian in the Austrian Parliament. In 1903, using the pseudonym Rudolf Springer, he published the book *Der Kampf der österreichischen Nationen um den Staat. Teil I: Das nationale Problem als Verfassungs- und Verwaltungsfrage.* Together with two later books from 1904 and 1906, this is still considered standard reading, basic to an understanding of the internal politics of the double monarchy and of the difficulties facing succeeding governments with respect to the national minorities.

The basic premise for Renner's proposal for reorganising the state was that it was a spiritual and cultural fellowship and not a material and economic association. By separating questions of culture from questions of federal state responsibilities, especially economics, defense and foreign policy, he hoped to reduce "the national question" to its cultural basis. Renner's proposal, which was later used in the Mährian and Ruthenian compromise in 1905 and in 1925 in Estland, combined definitions of nation on the basis of subjective political criteria with definitions of nation based on objective cultural criteria. The exact details seem excessively complicated today, but the main point is truly simple. Renner distinguished between *personal* affiliation with a cultural nation, represented across provincial boundaries, and *territorial* representation of all inhabitants in a region, regardless of nationality.

Soviet-Marxist concepts of nationality

Stalin criticised Renner in a book that was later to become the official blueprint for the nationality policy of the Soviet Union. The young Georgian upstart was in 1912 by Lenin sent on a study tour to the Austrian marxists in Vienna to gather ammunition for the theoretical discussions in the Second International. This resulted in a book by Stalin in which he criticised Renner and not least Bauer for having ignored the territorial basis of nations. To do so, Stalin pointed out, was only correct if one could solely conceive of one kind of territorial existence of a nation, the bourgeois national state. After having refuted Bauer's definition of the nation based on national character, Stalin continued:

> *"The nation is not simply a historical category, but a historical category from a certain epoch, the epoch of rising capitalism. The process that liquidated feudalism and developed capitalism at the same time joined people together as nations. This is the case, for example, in Western Europe. The English, French, Germans, Italians, etc. joined together to form nations, when victorious capitalism triumphantly took over from the divided world of feudalism. (...) The bourgeoisie played the lead (in creating the nation, U.Ø.). The most important question for the young bourgeoisie is the market. Its aim is to dispense of its goods and win in the competition with the bourgeoisie of other nationalities. This is the origin of its desire to ensure its "own", "home" market. The market is the first school where the bourgeoisie learns nationalism. (...) The nation has the right freely to determine its own destiny. It has the right to organise itself at its own pleasure, naturally without trespassing on the rights of other nations..."[7]*

The Bolsheviks' criticism of the Austrian marxists was two-fold. On the one hand, they criticised them for limiting the self-determination of nations by supporting a superior, multi-national state. On the other hand, the Austrian marxists were criticised on the grounds of their conserving undesirable national feelings through their federal arrangements. If Lenin could not get them with the one argument, Stalin would with the other. Realising this, it is not easy to avoid crowing over the problems which the Soviet state has run into lately with its un resolved national conflicts. But this is hardly fair. During all the outrage at the emotional form of debate used in the Second and Third Internationals, it must not be forgotten that the Soviet Union has actually administered the inheritance from the Czar's regime with more respect for national and cultural differences than most other regimes have managed to administer theirs. The Soviet empire has broken down because of economic difficulties, not because of its policy in the nationality question.

Bauer's Austrian Social Democratic principle of nationality

Renner hoped, perhaps naively, that his programme would transform economically based friction into cultural and legal discussions among educated citizens; this would preserve the German cultural influence in Southeast Europe, only without the oppression it had built upon under the Habsburgs. It was entirely in key, therefore, that during World War I Renner, a right-wing Social Democrat, concurred with the plans of Friedrich Naumanns (1860-1919), a liberal German politician, to create a German dominated federation in Central Europe, and battled against the left-wing, led by Otto bauer, who advocated a programme of national liberation.

Otto Bauer (1882-1938), who all his life belonged to the non-communist left-wing of SPÖ and was one of the most original Marxist theoreticians ever, in 1907 drafted the second epoch-making work on the question of nationality in Marxist theory. His intent was not so much to come up with practical proposals to reform Austria-Hungary as it was to create a theoretical basis for the policy of the Austrian Social Democrats on nationality. In contrast to Karl Kautsky (1854-1938), who without restrains advocated the nation-state, Bauer confessed that he "conceded to the reality of national fellowship" precisely in order to "be able to pursue our international policy".

Bauer saw the multi-national Austria-Hungary as an exception in the epoch of the national state, but an exception that was viable because the individual people's interest in the common market overshadowed their national craving for independence. For the same reason he championed the opinion of Rosa Luxemburg (1890-1919) that Poland ought to remain part of the Union with Russia. But in contrast with Luxemburg, he also advocated the principle of cultural autonomy under socialism – while she wanted to prohibit anything that created differences among people, including their nationality. From 1914, for tactical reasons, Lenin advocated national liberation to promote the revolution. Hovever, he gave up the demand as soon as the Bolsheviks had consolidated their power in 1920. In contrast, Bauer really believed in what he said about cultural autonomy even after the dissolution of capitalism. He argued for the desirability of a socialist state over other states in order to create the United States of Europe. The theoretical basis for all this Bauer took from the work of the German sociologist Ferdinand Tönnies (1855-1936). Ferdinand Tönnies contrasted *Gemeinschaft* with *Gesellschaft* as an alternative to the West European habit of identifying state with nation.

One can castigate both Bauer and Renner for lacking a sense of reality, and it has been done frequently, by the "superrealist" Communists among others, with whom they disagreed, and by later "realist", non-socialist historians and sociologists. However, the work of Bauer and Renner represents one of the few serious attempts to integrate the subjective and objective definitions of nation. Furthermore, they were men with real political power, who ran the risk eventually to have to live with the consequences of their ideas.

The concept of nationality in fascism and nazism

The most extreme logical consequence of the various concepts of nations surfaced in their undiluted forms in Fascist Italy and Nazi Germany, respectively. The objective definition of nationality and "race" in *Mein Kampf* and its subsequent consequences in the Nürnberg laws are infamous. What is less well known is the fact that, at least until the race laws of 1938, Italian Fascism built upon the opposed political-subjective principle of nationality.

According to Italian Fascist ideology, Croatians, Slovenians, Germans, Jews, and even Arabs and Ethiopians could be assimilated into Italian culture in Mussolini's new empire, just as they had been in the Roman empire. Political-moral accept based on common historic identity, not "the purity of blood" was the Fascist criterion for national belonging. It stood – at least in theory – in the sharpest contrast possible to the principles of race in Hitler's state. An intense propaganda war was waged between the two regimes up till 1936, from the Italian side through the association *Società per l'universalità di Roma*, founded in the summer 1933. Through this association, the Italians sought to spread their culture to non-Italians, especially in the Mediterranean region. This effort was opposed to the racist tendencies within the Fascist party and only lost out, because Mussolini needed support from his ideological companion north of the Alps to cope with the embargo that followed in the wake of the invasion of Ethiopia in 1935. Until 1938, when anti-Semitic (and anti-Hamitic) race laws were introduced in Italy, and the state shifted from a political-historic to a cultural-biological definition of nation, Mussolini ridiculed Nazi race theories with the statement that according to them, the Laplanders were probably the highest ranking of all races. Being himself a representative of Mediterranean civilisation Mussolini could not imagine anything more stupid and unreasonable.

The heritage from the 19th Century

This is the inheritance from the theoretical debates of the 19th century. Both definitions are still with us and have exercised enormous influence in the nation-states of today. This can be illustrated by a quick glance at the arbitrary criteria of the League of Nations and the UN for recognition of state independency. The difficulties in combining the two principles in the case of the modern state of Israel are startling – is a "Jew" a believer in the Mosaic faith, someone who has been brought up in Jewish cultural tradition, someone who considers himself a Jew, or, as the Nazis and fundamentalist Jews believe, anyone related to the Jewish "nation" through ancestry, marriage or biological ties? The complexity and intensity of the debate on this one issue alone, clearly demonstrates that this is not a dead issue. Unfortunately. The principles are mutually exclusive and a choice between the subjective-political defintition and the objective-cultural definition has to be made by all askiring "new" nations as well as by the older already "established" nations. A nation is an imagined community that has to be taught and reinforced by daily plebiscites, as Ernest Renan and N.F.S. Grundtvig put it in the last century.

Notes

1. "La constitution de 1795, tout comme ses ainées, est faite pour l' *homme* . Or, il n'y a point d' *homme* dans le monde. J'ai vu, dans ma vie, des Francais, des Italiens, des Russes, etc., je sais même, grace à Montesqieu, *qu'on peut ètre Persan:* mais quant à l'*homme,* je déclare ne l'avoir rencontré de ma vie; s'il existe, c'est bien á mon insu." J. de Maistre: *Oeuvres Complètes I ,,* Lille, 1891, p. 74.
2. Letter to Jessie White Mario, 23.3. 1857, quoted in Denis Mack Smith: *Il Risorgimento II ,,* Bari, 1968, p. 422.
3. E. Renan: *Oeuvres Complètes I ,* 1947, p. 893. A generation earlier, N.F.S. Grundtvig had put it lucidly in the song *"Folkeligt skal alt nu være"* (Let everything be of the people from now on), printed in: *"Danskeren" ,* 30.8.1848, no. 24, whose fourth stanza in the *"Højskolesangbogen"* is as follows: "Til et folk de alle høre/som sig egne selv dertil/ har for modersmålet øre/ har for fædrelandet ild/...". (To one people belong all those/who count themselves there/ have an ear for the mother tongue/ and burn for the fatherland).This is a surprisingly early formulation of Renan's political-subjective principle. Cf. U. Østergård: *"Bønder og danskere",* 1988, and Vagn Wåhlin: *"Ikke stykkevis og delt" ,* 1986, particularly pp. 44-46.
4. Renan in a letter to the German historian David Friedrich Strauss, quoted in Alain Finkielkraut: *La défaite de la pensée ,* 1987, p. 40.
5. Renan 1882 in *Oeuvres Compèltes I ,* 1947, p. 902, 903 og 904.
6. Karl Renner was elected chancellor in the first Austrian republic 1919 to 1920. Imprisoned by the conservatives in 1934 he survived World War II in concentration camp and presided over the establishment of the second Austrian republic 1945-50 as president.
7. J.V. Stalin: *Marxismus und nationale Frage* (1913), *Werke 2 ,* 1953, p. 266-333. The article was written in Vienna at the end of 1912 and in early 1913 and printed in 1913 in nos. 3-5 of the Bolshevik journal *Prosvesjtsjenije* (Enlightenment). In 1914 it was published as a pamphlet. 1920 printed in Stalin's *"Articles"* on the question of nationalism, setting the official policy of the party towards minorities in the Soviet Union. Cf. E.H. Carr: *The Bolshevik Revolution I ,* 1950, p. 426.

References

This booklist contains only works quoted in the text and in the notes. A more elaborate list of references to recent research and scholarly debate on the subject can be found in U. Østergård: *Hvad er en nationstat?* 1988.

Bauer, Otto. 1907. *Die Nationalitätenfrage und die Sozialdemokratie,* Marx Studien Vol. II, Wien.
Carr, E. H. 1950. *The Bolshevik Revolution I.* Penguin.
Finkielkraut, Alain. 1987. *La défaite de la pensée.* Paris.
North Atlantic Studies vol. 1, no. 1,. 1989.
Maistre, Joseph Ernest. 1914. "Considérations sur la France". In: *Oeuvres Complètes I.* Lille 1891.
Renan, Ernest. 1882. "Qu'est-ce qu'une nation? Oeuvres Complètes I, Paris 1947, pp. 887-906.
Renner, Karl (Rudolf Springer). 1903. *Der Kampf der österreichischen Nationen um den Staat.* Wien.
Smith, Denis Mack. 1968. *Il Risorgimento vol. II.* Bari.
Stalin, J.V. 1913. *Marxismus un nationale Frage. Werke II.*
Wåhlin, Vagn. 1986. "Ikke stykkevis og delt". In: Becker-Nielsen (ed.), *Stykkevis og delt. 5 essays om Grundtvig og grundtvigianisme.* Aarhus. pp. 9-52.
Weber, Eugen. 1976. *Peasants into Frenchmen, Stanford.*
Østergård, Uffe. 1988. "Bønder og danskere". In: Vagn Wåhlin (ed.), *Historien i kulturhistorien.* Aarhus. pp. 317-371.
Østergård, Uffe. 1988. *Hvad er en nationstat?* Aarhus.

Linguicism:

A tool for analysing linguistic inequality and promoting linguistic human rights

Tove Skutnabb-Kangas and Robert Phillipson

ABSTRACT
The paper presents the concept *linguicism,* which has structural and ideological components. Linguicism is exemplified in relation to two areas, the global hegemony of English, and dominated indigenous and immigrated languages in Europe and Europeanised countries. The need for an international declaration of linguistic human rights, as one of the ways of combating linguicism, is demonstrated. Existing international or "universal" convenants do not guarantee the promotion of minority languages that they need, a promotion that speakers of dominant languages take for granted for themselves.

Introducing linguicism[1]

Just as colonialism has been superseded by more sophisticated forms of exploitation, crudely biological racist ideology (see Miles 1989) has been superseded by ethnicism (see Mullard 1988) and linguicism (Phillipson & Skutnabb-Kangas 1986a). The presumed superiority of the West – "white", middle class, male – is now less represented by the gun and the bible than by technology and the textbook. Internationally, English is spreading and being consolidated as one element of a process of Western cultural diffusion worldwide, with major implications for other languages. Nationally, some of the "English-speaking" states increasingly acknowledge the de facto diversity linguistic diversity in their midst, while others are attempting to stamp it out. The "English Only" movement in the USA shows members of the dominant group using language as a means of attempting to ensure cultural homogeneity (for a denunciation see Fishman 1989).

Sociologists are often suspicious of an emphasis on language when discussing the strategies oppressed groups can use to obtain more power. Many seem to think that a focus on language and culture is introduced by dominant groups so as to fool the dominated into ignoring the more substantial questions of economic and political power (see for example Castles 1987). Language questions may indeed have been used like this in some contexts, but the suspicion may be unfounded. A more substantial problem is the relative scarcity of interdisciplinary efforts in this area, possibly combined with a failure to appreciate the significance of language and linguistic hierarchisation. One aim of this paper is to demonstrate how the study of language can be of significance to scholars interested in the empowering of minorities.

A central concept which we have developed is *linguicism,* "the ideologies and structures which are used to legitimate, effectuate and reproduce an unequal division of power and resources (both material and non-material) between groups which are defined on the basis of language" (Skutnabb-Kangas 1986, 1988, Phillipson 1988). Linguicism is similar in its workings and effects to racism, sexism, classism, ageism and similar structures and ideologies which serve to maintain inequality. Like these, linguicism can operate at both the individual and the societal levels. The *structural* foundations on which linguistic inequality rests can be traced in the relative power and the economic support accruing to different languages in specific, concrete institutions (courts of law, bureaucracies, schools, media, etc). Provision for these is enshrined in laws and regulations which regulate, explicitly or implicitly, the rights of languages and speakers of languages. The *ideologies* which legitimate the dominance of one language over others can be seen in beliefs and values in relation to different languages. The structures and ideologies interlock in informing the language-related practices of such key spheres as schools and universities, of "aid" organisations, business and administration, the media, etc.

The workings of linguicism, and the ways in which it interacts with other inequitable structures and ideologies, are as yet relatively under-explored. The theoretical construct, linguicism, can be used in empirical studies of how linguistic inequality is structurally determined, how it is ideologically legitimated and how it has been contested. We would claim that linguicism operates in any situation, nationally or internationally, in which one language dominates at the expense of others. Study of linguicism can also serve as a springboard on which to project strategies for contesting such inequality, delegitimating it, and ultimately obtaining more justice for speakers of dominated languages.

The documentation of the articulation of linguicism can be analysed in conjunction with a theory of language and imperialism (Phillipson 1990). English has been the imperialist language par excellence of the past two centuries – a language of wider colonisation as we call it, rather than the euphemism, "a language of wider communication". In some of our earlier work we have studied the history of the entrenchment of English and the arguments used for legitimating its spread in the post-colonial world, in particular its function as the language of power and as a bridgehead for Western interests in underdeveloped countries (Phillipson & Skutnabb-Kangas 1986b). The concept linguicism has also been evolved in the analysis of minority education (Skutnabb-Kangas 1984a, 1988). In this paper we shall exemplify linguicism in relation to two areas, the global hegemony of English, and dominated indigenous and immigrated languages in Europe and Europeanised countries. We demonstrate the need for an international declaration of linguistic human rights, as one of the ways of combating linguicism.

The international linguistic hegemony of English

One part of Western "civilisation" is its languages[2]. Although empire is now largely vestigial, one of its most enduring legacies is language. The global spread of English has gone through several phases, as the hegemony of English has adapted to a constantly evolving situation. In the colonialist phase, the white man's linguistic burden was imposed as the dominant language throughout a far-flung empire. In the neocolonial phase of the past quarter century, the "development" message has been carried overseas through the medium of the "international" language, English. Native speakers of British and American English, and "experts" using English as a second language, whether in overt business or in "aid", in person or on celluloid, have served to secure the establishment or perpetuation of linguistic bridgeheads throughout the global periphery. In "independent" Third World countries the position of English has been consolidated, both for internal and external purposes. The language has taken on new identities, and linguicism ensures its predominance.

To put things more metaphorically, whereas once *Britannia ruled the waves,* now it is English which rules them. The British empire has given way to the empire of English. English is seen very widely as providing access to employment, influence, desirable goods, etc. In Kachru's phrase (1986, 1), the linguistic power of English is an alchemy:

> *"English is considered a symbol of modernization, a key to expanded functional roles, and an extra arm for success and mobility in culturally and linguistically complex and pluralistic societies... (English) permits one to open the linguistic gates to international business, technology, science, and travel."*

The elites in underdeveloped countries owe their position in part to their proficiency in English, and therefore accord a high priority to the learning of English. Even those not proficient in the language can see what it does for those who are, as evidence from oppressed groups in the Third World shows, whether peasants in Kenya (Obura 1986, 421) or slum-dwellers in Bombay, where the English medium school is a prestige symbol (Rajyashree 1986, 46).

Those who fail in the quest for the alchemy of English see their life chances reduced. Those who become proficient in the alien language may sacrifice the language of their parents and their own culture in the process. The dominant language partially displaces other languages, through exclusive use of the language in certain domains (for instance in the media, or in the "modern" sector of the economy and in administration), and may replace the other languages totally (Phillipson & Skutnabb-Kangas 1986b). Linguicism in the form of excessive reliance on the former colonial language has ensured that indigenous languages have been excluded from the "modernisation" process. The invariable corollary of the high status of English has been the low status of other languages. This false either-or dichotomy is based on an ideology of monolingualism as the desired societal norm. An ideology of multilingualism would lead to a development of both or several languages. Linguicism, in one of its concrete forms as foreign "aid", has assured the channelling of resources to the European language and the starvation of local languages. In many parts of the world linguicist structures and processes have resulted not in English enriching other languages and cultures but in English supplanting them.

There is an acute awareness of the *economic, political, linguistic, educational and psychological costs* of linguicist policies among many researchers in the underdeveloped countries. English is seen in India as one of the major symbols of "Indian intellectual slavery" (Pattanayak 1986, 29). Kahombo Mateene, the director of the recently scrapped Inter-African Bureau of Languages of the OAU, one of the most vocal critics of the overuse of former colonial languages in Africa, having shown that colonial languages are now used more than during the colonial times, likewise says that "...colonial languages keep Africans in slavery which remains yet to be got rid of" (1980). Enriquez & Protacio Marcelino (1984,3) see "the continued use of English and, with it, an American-oriented curriculum as psychologically and politically inimical to the nationalist and democratic aspirations of the Filipino people. It undermines Filipino values and orientation and perpetuates the miseducation and captivity of the minds of the Filipino people to the colonial outlook. It lowers the Filipinos' defenses against continued American economic and cultural aggression. An educational system was produced that contravenes democratic ideals by providing quality education for the rich but mediocre education for the poor. It also fosters further regionalism and obstructs national unity."

We have analysed elsewhere the illegitimacy of many of the arguments used to ensure the continued dominance of English (Skutnabb-Kangas & Phillipson 1986b, Phillipson 1990). They tend to focus on the present – e.g. the availability of books in one language, or teachers trained to operate in that language – and thereby to ignore the potential of indigenous languages. English tends to be marketed as a tool or instrument, as though this can be divorced from the Western worldview that the language embodies or the interests of those who are able to operate in the language. It is in fact only a tiny proportion of the population in underdeveloped countries where English is projected as a language of "national unity" who can use English. We have analysed the illegitimate arguments under three headings: "English-intrinsic" (what English "is"), "English-extrinsic" (what English "has") and "English-functional" (what English "can do"). The arguments are used to ensure the continued allocation of resources to activities which entrench English and hinder the growth of indigenous languages.

This legitimation has affinities with the way racism is affirmed (Preiswerk 1980). It involves *self-exaltation* on the part of the dominant language, *degradation* of the dominated languages, and *rationalisation* of the relationship between them. The dominant group/language presents an idealized image of itself (it is modern, developed, ideologically neutral; it *has* teachers, materials, literature, dictionaries; skills, know-how via its experts). The dominant group/language stigmatizes the dominated groups/languages, for instance by labelling them primitive or traditional. And they rationalize the relationship between the two, always to the advantage of the dominant group/language. This is done through convincing-sounding arguments about the benefits for speakers of "minor" languages from using the dominant language. This is marketed by reference to everything it can "do" for speakers of other languages. The rationalisation also includes projecting the monolingualism of the dominant language group as the norm, instead of accepting the fact that a majority of the world's population is in fact multilingual.

There is also an acute awareness of *alternatives* to the present linguicist policy, an awareness that it is only by using indigenous languages that the essential needs of the mass of people in underdeveloped countries can be met, whether in the Philippines (Enriquez & Protacio Marcelino 1984), Algeria (Kateb Yacine 1989) or Kenya (Ngugi 1986). "The medium of instruction must be free from any association with domination", as Mateene puts it (1980). Ngugi writes in "Decolonising the Mind" (1986, xiv):

"This book...is my farewell to English as a vehicle for any of my writings. From now on it is Gikuyu and Kiswahili all the way. However, I hope that through the age old medium of translation I shall be able to continue dialogue with all." His justification is that: "In the eighteenth and nineteenth centuries Europe stole art, treasures from Africa to decorate their houses and museums; in the twentieth century Europe is stealing the treasures of the mind to enrich their languages and cultures. Africa needs back its economy, its politics, its culture, its languages and all its patriotic writers." (ibid., xii).

Linguicism in relation to indigenous and immigrated minority languages

The monolingualism ideology provides a legitimation for killing other languages, through active linguocide or through passivity, letting other languages die. Educational provision is one of the central agencies in this linguicist process. If majority languages were treated as additional languages which were to be learned in addition to minority mother tongues, the linguistic goal of education would, at least for minority language speakers, be bilingualism. If minority languages were accorded the same value as majority languages, they would be maintained, and thus the educational goal would, at least for minority language speakers, also be bilingualism. Instead, in all the educational systems organised for virtually all minority children in all European and Europeanised countries, the main thrust of language learning is on the learning of the majority language by the minority children. Bilingualism in school should be about learning two languages, but the part which has to do with the minority language tends to be conveniently forgotten. The result is that minority languages are killed, through lack of adequate support. Education has, through its linguicist and culturist policies, succeeded much better than the brutal physical force of slavery and colonial times in wiping out languages, cultures and peoples (see for instance Deirdre Jordan's convincing analysis of the comparable educational experience of Canadian Inuit, Nordic Same and Australian aboriginal indigenous groups (1988)). It also seems to be succeeding with the present immigrant generation, the "great grandchildren" of slaves and colonised people (see Skutnabb-Kangas 1984a, Cummins 1984, and contributions to Skutnabb-Kangas & Cummins (eds) 1988).

The results of forced linguistic and cultural assimilation on minorities, both indigenous and immigrated, are well known. Linguistic minority children are grossly overrepresented among those who do not attend schools at all, those who experience difficulty at school, are placed in ESN (=educationally sub-normal) classes, who drop out, leave school with no formal qualifications, and, after school, are unemployed. Several kinds of deficiency theories have been used in order to explain the difficulties. The children, their parents, their group and their language and culture have been declared deficient, as a handicap, as a hindrance to success to be compensated for and abandoned. Another way has been to make the language and cultures of minorities invisible. "Language" means the majority language. Minority children are defined negatively (in terms of what they are NOT or do NOT know, instead of what they are and do know). In addition they are defined in relation to their knowledge – or supposed lack of knowledge – of the majority language. Thus they are called NEP or LEP children (No/Low English Proficiency) as in the USA, NESB (Non-English Speaking Background), as in Australia, or "fremmedsproget" (= "foreign-speaking") as in Denmark.

Most of those sociologists who have explained the low degree of school achievement among minority children as a result of unequal power relationships have nevertheless failed to see how schools have reflected and reinforced those power relationships through their language policies. Colonial physical force has been replaced by neocolonial economic policies and, increasingly, by colonising the mind. The means have shifted from sticks to carrots to ideas (Galtung 1980). Likewise, the physical separation from parents and the punishment for speaking the mother tongue of earlier times have been replaced by the sophisticated practices of intercultural (multicultural) education, which in fact deprives minority children both of their languages and their cultures, as well as the education which they would have been entitled to, under the cover of well-meaning enrichment for all; see Skutnabb-Kangas 1988 for an analysis of the different phases in the diagnosis of the reasons for minority children's educational failure, and the corresponding measures implemented in each phase.

Majority language speakers enjoy the exercise of linguistic human rights, often without being conscious of doing so, as these rights are so self-evident. It is minority language speakers who have to struggle for equivalent rights. In their struggle against linguicism they need to know what support there is for linguistic human rights in national legislation or international covenants.

Universal declaration of 'Linguistic Human Rights' needed

From a linguistic point of view all languages in the world have the same worth. All are logical, cognitively complex, and capable of expressing any thoughts, provided enough resources are devoted to cultivation. There are no such things as "primitive languages". On linguistic grounds all languages could have the same rights, the same possibility of being learned fully, developed and used in all situations by their speakers. The political rights or lack of rights cannot be deduced from linguistic considerations. They can only be understood in their historical context as results of the processes which have led to the present division of power and resources in the societies concerned.

The majority of the world's fewer than 200 states are officially monolingual, while they harbour speakers of some 4-5000 languages. Languages which are not official do not have the same rights which official languages have. Official state monolingualism means that in most countries all the minorities are linguistically oppressed, and their linguistic human rights are violated. But instead of this being admitted and analysed as the oppression it is, the ideology of linguicism legitimates linguistic oppression.

In an attempt to systematise and review language-related rights, especially in education, we have devised a grid, charting some of the important dimensions of language rights. We have represented linguistic assimilation into the dominant language group and the maintenance of a minority language, processes which the state cannot directly regulate through laws and decrees, as goals and results of the different rights or lack of rights. The dimensions we use are degree of overtness and degree of promotion. Both are seen as continua. If the minority languages, or the languages of powerless majorities, for instance in African countries where English or French are the dominant languages in education, are not mentioned at all in regulations about schooling, this would represent a point close to the "covert" end of the continuum. If exactly how many hours per week a language is to be taught as a subject is laid down, this would be close to the "overt" end.

The promotion continuum starts with *prohibition* of a language – which is obviously strongly assimilation-oriented. It continues via *toleration*, where the language is not forbidden (explicitly or implicitly), to *non-discrimination prescription*, where discrimination of people on the basis of language is forbidden. The next point is *permission* to use the minority language, and at the other end of the continuum we have *promotion* of it, oriented towards maintaining it.

In our earlier studies (Skutnabb-Kangas & Phillipson 1986a, 1989) we have reviewed a sample of inter-

Figure 1: Language Rights in Selected Covenants

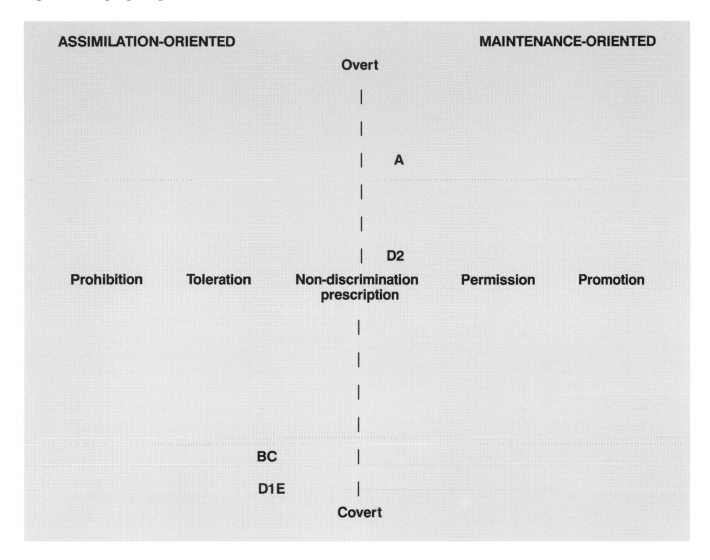

national and European conventions and decrees. The following have been plotted onto the grid in figure 1:-

A: *The Charter of the United Nations 1945,*
B: *The Universal Declaration of Human Rights 1948,*
C: *International Covenant on Economic, Social and Cultural Rights 1966,*
D1:*The UN Declaration of Children's Rights 1959 (and D2: the new Draft Convention on the Rights of the Child, 1988),*
E: *The Council of Europe Convention for the Protection of Human Rights and Fundamental Freedoms 1950; we have omitted European Parliament resolutions with no legal force in individual countries.*

In the same studies we have also reviewed the extent to which a number of national constitutions guarantee linguistic human rights (Finland, India, Yugoslavia, etc; the proposed English Language Amendments to the US Constitution fall squarely within prohibition, with varying degrees of overtness).

On the basis of the review of international covenants we conclude that no legally binding declarations are mother-tongue maintenance oriented. None of them comes further than to overt non-discrimination prescription. In fact, most of them only require covert toleration of minority mother tongues. Our studies show that not even overt maintenance-oriented permission is enough for minority (or powerless majority) mother tongues to be maintained and developed. What minority languages require is *overt maintenance-oriented promotion.* This necessarily includes the allocation of the economic means for supporting mother tongue medium schools – one of the crucial deficiencies in Unesco's Convention against Discrimination in Education. Most existing declarations tend to be too vague and conceptually confused, and both the right of redress and the economic prerequisites for using the rights have been deficient.

Thus a central conclusion is that *the existing international or "universal" declarations are in no way adequate to provide support for dominated languages.* The evidence unmistakably shows that while individuals and groups are supposed to enjoy "cultural" and "social" rights, linguistic human rights are neither guaranteed nor protected, i.e. *structural linguicism is also reflected in all the international declarations.* In order to combat linguicism and institutional discrimination, in education and elsewhere, against minority language children, there is a need for legislation which explicitly promotes minority languages within a maintenance-oriented framework.

At an international seminar on Human Rights and Cultural Rights (7-9.10.1987 in Recife, Brazil) organised by AIMAV (the International Association for Cross-cultural Communication) and Unesco, a Declaration of Recife was adopted. The preamble ends as follows:

> "Hence, conscious *of the need to provide explicit legal guarantees for linguistic rights to individuals and groups by the appropriate bodies of the member states of the United Nations,*
> *RECOMMENDS that steps be taken by the United Nations to adopt and implement a UNIVERSAL DECLARATION OF LINGUISTIC RIGHTS which would require a reformulation of national, regional, and international language policies."*

A preliminary Declaration ("RESOLUTION ON LINGUISTIC RIGHTS"/ "RESOLUCAO SOBRE DIREITOS LINGUISTICOS)" was also adopted by the Seminar. It is based on our provisional declaration (Skutnabb-Kangas 1984b):

> "1. *Every social group has the right to positively identify with one or more languages and to have such identification accepted and respected by others*
> 2. *Every child has the right to learn the language(s) of his/her group fully*
> 3. *Every person has the right to using the language(s) of his/her group in any official situation*
> 4. *Every person has the right to learn fully at least one of the official languages in the country where s/he is resident, according to her/his own choice."*

There was a follow-up gathering at UNESCO in Paris in April 1989, organized by FIPLV, the Federation Internationale des Professeurs de Langues Vivantes, as a result of which a revised, expanded document is being circulated to a substantial number of professional associations and researchers, and the elaborate machinery for processing such a declaration is being set in motion. The exercise will involve a major task for the scientific community in clarifying concepts, drawing international comparisons, and elaborating a declaration of universal relevance and applicability.

One issue that has yet to be clarified is whether the right to learn *foreign* languages will be included. There are considerable pressures afoot in Europe at present to ensure that all European children learn two foreign languages at school. The LINGUA and ERASMUS programmes are designed to implement such a policy, and the disagreement between Britain and its European partners (Britain has refused to agree on a policy of two foreign languages in schools) reflects a major difference in perception of the issues. The British insularly assume that the dominant position of English internationally is in their interest. Continental European countries wish to ensure that their children learn English and one other language – French/German/Spanish/etc, i.e. the dominant languages of two neighbouring European countries. This reflects the wish of Europeans to provide a counterweight to the pervasive influence of English and to bolster the official languages of other European countries.

There is a significant difference, however, between the need of dominated minority languages for protection in order to ensure their survival and basic justice on the one hand, and the urge to promote European unity through multilingualism for "international understanding" on the other. It is undoubtedly a human right to learn one's mother tongue, a right that speakers of the dominant language take for granted for themselves. Is it though, in the contemporary world, a human right to learn several languages in school? A variety of answers is possible to this question, reflecting the complexity of the issues involved. We can only hope that disagreement about the scope of linguistic human rights will not delay the elaboration of a declaration which provides substantial guarantees for dominated ethnolinguistic minority languages.

The recent Draft Universal Declaration on Indigenous Rights (as contained in document E/CN.4/Sub.2/1988/25) is a pointer in the right direction, as it establishes as fundamental human rights that indigenous peoples should have

> "9. *The right to maintain and use their own languages, including for administrative, judicial and other relevant purposes.*
> 10. *The right to all forms of education, including in particular the right of children to have access to education in their own languages, and to establish, structure, conduct and control their own educational systems and institutions.*
> 23. *The collective right to autonomy in matters relating to their own internal and local affairs, including education, information, culture, religion, health, housing, social welfare, traditional and other economic activities, land and resources administration and the environment, as well as internal taxation for financing these autonomous functions."*

The international community thus appreciates that the linguistic human rights of indigenous peoples should be promoted. Very few ethnolinguistic minorities enjoy such rights at present, meaning that linguistic human rights are violated. Hence the need for a *Universal Declaration of Linguistic Human Rights.*

Linguistic human rights are blatantly violated in the educational systems in every country in the world. Groups defined on the basis of their mother tongues thus get unequal access to educational resources, i.e. these educational systems reflect linguicism. An awareness of linguicism as a fact is the first step towards starting to find ways of combating it and empowering dominated groups. This awareness benefits from an analysis of the relationship between racism and linguicism, and of the increasingly sophisticated ways in which these operate.

Notes

1. This article is a revised version of two papers, one given at the Aarhus *Greenland* conference on 27 October 1989, and an earlier one at the Conference on New Frontiers in Social Research, held by the International Sociological Association, Research Committee on Ethnic, Race and Minority Relations at the Centre for Race and Ethnic Studies, University of Amsterdam, The Netherlands, December 1988. A slightly modified version has appeared in the *Journal of Group Tensions*, 1990 volume.
2. On the genesis of Spanish imperial language policy see Illich 1981. On French imperial language policy see Calvet 1974 and 1987. Calvet's use of the term "linguistic racism", when referring to the glorification of the dominant language and stigmatisation of other languages, has clear affinities to our concept *linguicism*.

References:

Annamalai, E., Björn Jernudd & Joan Rubin (eds) 1986. *Language Planning, Proceedings of an Institute*. Mysore & Honolulu: Central Institute of Indian Languages & East-West Center.

Calvet, Louis-Jean 1974. *Linguistique et colonialisme: petit traite de glottophagie*. Paris: Payot.

Calvet, Louis-Jean 1987. *La guerre des langues et les politiques linguistiques*. Paris: Payot.

Castles Stephen 1987. *The role of social sciences in the construction of ethnic minorities in Australia*. Paper for the Conference "Der Beitrag der Wissenschaften zur Konstitution etnischer Minderheiten", Zentrum für interdiziplinäre Forschung, Universität Bielefeld, 13-16 September 1987 (in press).

Centre of African Studies 1986. *Language in education in Africa*. Seminar proceedings 26, proceedings of a seminar at the Centre of African Studies, University of Edinburgh, 29-30 November 1985. Edinburgh: Centre of African Studies.

Cummins, Jim 1984. *Bilingualism and special education: Issues in assessment and pedagogy*. Clevedon: Multilingual Matters 6.

Enriquez, Virgilio G. and Elizabeth Protacio Marcelino 1984. *Neo-Colonial Policies and the Language Struggle in the Phillippines*. Quezon City: Phillippine Psychology Research and Training House.

Fishman, Joshua A 1989. "Bias and anti-intellectualism: the frenzied fiction of 'English Only'". in J.A.Fishman *Language and ethnicity in minority sociolinguistic perspective*. Clevedon: Multilingual Matters.

Illich, Ivan 1981. "Taught mother language and vernacular tongue". in D.P.Pattanayak *Multilingualism and mother tongue education*. Delhi: Oxford University Press, 1-39.

Jordan, Deirdre F. 1988. "Rights and claims of indigenous people: Education and the reclaiming of identity. The case of the Canadian Natives, thc Sami and Australian Aborigines". in Skutnabb-Kangas & Cummins (eds) 1988, 189-222.

Kachru, Braj B. 1986. *The alchemy of English: the spread, functions and models of non-native Englishes*. Oxford: Pergamon.

Kateb, Yacine 1989. As reported in *The Guardian Weekly*. Nov. 26.

Mateene, Kahombo 1980a. "Failure in the obligatory use of European languages in Africa and the advantages of a policy of linguistic independence" in Mateene & Kalema (eds) 1980, 9-41.

Mateene, Kahombo & John Kalema (eds.) 1980. *Reconsideration of African linguistic policies*. Kampala: OAU Bureau of Languages. OAU/BIL Publication 3.

Miles, Robert 1989. *Racism*. London & New York: Routledge & Kegan Paul.

Mullard, Chris 1988. "Racism, ethnicism and etharcy or not? The principles of progressive control and transformative change" in Skutnabb-Kangas & Cummins (eds) 1988, 359-378.

Ngugi, Wa Thiong'o 1986. *Decolonising the Mind: the politics of language in African literature*. London: James Currey.

Obura, Anna P. 1986. "Research issues and perspectives in language in education in Africa: an agenda for the next decade" in *Centre of African Studies* 1986, 413-444.

Pattanayak, Debi Prasanna 1986. "Language, Politics, Region Formation, and Regional Planning" in Jernudd & Rubin (eds) *Annamalai*, 1986, 18-42.

Phillipson, Robert 1990. *English language teaching and imperialism*. Doctoral dissertation, University of Amsterdam. Tronninge, Denmark: Transcultura.

Phillipson, Robert 1988. "Linguicism: structures and ideologies in linguistic imperialism" in Skutnabb-Kangas & Cummins (eds) 1988, 339-358.

Phillipson, Robert & Tove Skutnabb-Kangas 1986a. *Linguicism rules in education*. Roskilde: Roskilde University Centre. 3 volumes.

Phillipson, Robert & Tove Skutnabb-Kangas 1986b. "English: the language of wider colonisation" in Phillipson & Skutnabb-Kangas 1986a, 344-377.

Preiswerk, Roy (ed) 1980. *The slant of the pen: racism in children's books*. Geneva: World Council of Churches.

Rajyashree, K.S. 1986. *An ethnolinguistic survey of Dharavi, a slum in Bombay*. Mysore: Central Institute of Indian Languages.

Skutnabb-Kangas, Tove 1984a. *Bilingualism or not – the education of minorities*. Clevedon: Multilingual Matters.

Skutnabb-Kangas, Tove 1984b. "Barns språkliga mänskliga rättigheter. Om finsk frigörelsekamp på den svenska skolfronten" (Children's linguistic human rights. On Finnish Liberation Struggle on the Swedish School Front) *Kritisk Psykologi* 1-2. 1984, 38-46.

Skutnabb-Kangas, Tove 1986. "Multilingualism and the education of minority children" in Phillipson & Skutnabb-Kangas 1986a, 42-72; also in Skutnabb-Kangas & Cummins (eds) 1988, 9-44.

Skutnabb-Kangas, Tove & Jim Cummins (eds) 1988. *Minority Education: from Shame to Struggle*. Clevedon: Multilingual Matters.

Skutnabb-Kangas, Tove & Robert Phillipson 1986a. "Denial of linguistic rights: the new mental slavery" in Phillipson & Skutnabb-Kangas 1986a, 416-465.

Skutnabb-Kangas, Tove & Robert Phillipson 1986b. "The legitimacy of the arguments for the spread of English" in Phillipson & Skutnabb-Kangas 1986a, 378-415.

Skutnabb-Kangas, Tove & Robert Phillipson 1989. *Wanted! Linguistic Human Rights*. ROLIG-Papir 44. Roskilde: Roskilde University Centre.

Indigenous Rights between Law and Sociology:

Internationalising soft norms in a hard context

Frederik Harhoff

ABSTRACT

The article identifies some of the aspects in dogmatic legal science, which are relevant to the study of binding norms beyond the traditional hierarchy of legal sources. As for the right of self-determination for indigenous peoples in international law, the article holds that recognition of this right in a legal regime will depend on the international community's willingness to accept modifications to the principle of state sovereignty.

Indigenous rights in a legal context

For every lawyer engaged in elaborating *the rights of indigenous peoples*, a serious problem of their legal context and character has supervened with inevitable force: Are Indigenous Rights legally binding rules or are they no more than sociological norms, and can they at all be considered on an international level? As it may be seen even from the way this question is posed, most practising lawyers would tend to consider sociological norms as not only subordinated to legal rules, but also void of any judiciable substance and therefore almost useless in a legal context. – Others would contend that Indigenous Rights are indeed inscribed in a number of both national and international legal instruments and therefore must be handled within the legal regime. Since both views seem to contain reasonable arguments, the legal world has remained uneasy on the issue and in the meantime, *Indigenous Rights* rest in limbo. In my view, however, the question whether Indigenous Rights belong to one or the other scientific regime, is wrongly posed. Many traditional concepts in International Law are yielding under the pressure for new explanations of the international structure, and it cannot be disputed that Indigenous Rights form part of the new trends in *"World Community Law"*. The relevant question, in other words, is not whether Indigenous Rights are legal in their character or not, but rather how to soften the concept and ecology of International Law so as to allow for a meaningful evaluation of Indigenous Rights in an international context.

It is in this perspective that the present article will try to illuminate some of the predominant elements in the *history and philosophy of law*, which have brought about the modern positions on Indigenous Rights.

The limits of dogmatic law

Within a traditional and dogmatic concept of law, a *legal right* is generally understood as having a content which is *judiciable* through public procedural remedies and, at least in principle, *enforceable* through public sanctions. The model for legal analysis, in turn, is based on established traditions and adequate methodical instructions in *how to combine theory with its object*. Because of the legal system's particular affiliation with private proprietary rights, such methods are all well established for the traditional core of legal studies: the protection of private property and regulation of public authority. In the periphery around and outside this core, however, theoretical delimitations, scientific traditions and methodical approaches are much less evident. In the "grey areas" between Law, Sociology and Politics, no well-established codex of legal concepts and scientific models is immediately available for the legal analysis, and no adequate parameters have yet been identified for exchange and mutual use of scientific conclusions between legal science and other social or humanistic sciences. The problem, as it often appears before the individual lawyer who becomes absorbed in the elaboration of legal norms in such "grey areas", is really twofold:

First, neither prevailing legal science nor, for that matter, other related social or humanistic sciences, offer much help in how to *determine* and *perceive* behavioural norms or standards within such areas in a *legal* context. Above all, the established legal science and theories do *not* allow for immediate recognition and enforceability of "informal" rights or duties and other behaviourial norms, which govern the relations between subjects in humanitarian or controversial political areas.

Second, we have no adequate parameters for exchange of theoretical achievementswithin one scientific discipline to another; results reached in legal science are not directly transferable, or at best only hardly applicable, to other sciences where similar or comparable achievements may have been made. If the concept of Law remains unchanged and unchallenged, such rights as e.g., *indigenous rights* can hardly be proven to exist as true legal rights within a traditional and dogmatic legal regime, and may therefore face the risk of being disregarded by judicial and executive authorities. This is the effective problem which lawyers have to solve.

The importance of the (legal) language

Applying law in practice implies *association of a legal norm with certain particular and legally relevant facts*, which are preselected out of the entire complexity of circumstances in each individual case. – Reality is always composed of a vast multitude of detailed and irregular facts, some of which may be of, say, *sociological* interest and therefore particularly identified for a sociological study, while others could be of *cultural* interest (for an examination of cultural phenomena), and yet others are of particular *legal* interest for lawyers operating in a legal context – e.g. in determining the facts and sequence of actions during the proceedings of a case before the court, etc. Thus, each of the professional academics may identify and sort out very different facts from the same event and in doing so, *they constitute their own picture of reality*. The lawyer, in other words, preselects and presents the facts of an incident so as to make them fit into the standardized regime of the particular legal norm on which he pleads his case. By excluding "irrelevant" facts from the account of the case, the lawyer *shapes the actual reality in accordance with an ideological world-picture, common to the legal establishment*. Thus, the "true reality" is perceived as being neutrally reflected in the constructed "reality" produced by Law. The *legal language constitutes the formal expression of the way in which the legal profession perceives the relation between law and the legal subjects, their interests, their possessions, and the State.*

Although lawyers and e.g. anthropologists may study the same abstract problem and have the same goal in doing so, they do indeed speak a very different language and apply very different scientific methods. In building standards for the transfer of scientific results from one academic regime to another, we have to find ways to coordinate or unify related *linguistic* tools, because language, as we have seen, is the form in which the different world pictures with their different values and norms are expressed and transferred. This will become even more evident as we turn to the discourse between actors from *different cultures*.

Legal methodology and scientific interaction

The next problem to deal with is that of scientific methods. Traditional and dogmatic legal science is largely based on principles and methods adopted from the *positivist natural sciences*. The way in which lawyers *pose questions* and *define legal problems* is thus often governed by a mechanistic and functionalistic perception of how the world is composed and how it can be expounded, and defects eventually "fixed". Legal scientific methods apply the same basic quantitative criteria as those developed in natural science, including such demands to *accuracy, measurability, verification* and *predictability* as known from the natural sciences. Traditional legal science, in other words, will tend to exclude "soft" knowledge and facts which are not provable or reliable; this is exactly the reason why Law itself is thought to be distinguishable from the very facts to which Law is applied. Also on the metaphysical level, dogmatic legal arguments are based on the presumption that the *acting subject* is distinguishable from the *investigated object, facts* from *assessments, objective knowledge* from *subjective beliefs, causality* from *validity*, etc.

In dogmatic legal science, problems are always perceived and shaped in such a manner that they can be handled within the established methodical framework; new and very complex problems may of course be identified and dealt with, but only on certain premises which keep the whole manoeuvre well within the notorious legal world picture. Thus, scientific interaction between Law and other disciplines is not possible unless we expand the conceptual and methodical frameworks of Law so as to allow for the inclusion of evaluative premises in the legal analysis.

Modernity and the distinction between subject and object

This distinction in traditional dogmatic law between subject and object originally stems from the shift in paradigm introduced by the *Era of Enligthment* in the middle of the 18th century. The preceding century's Christian Reformation and the subsequent Renaissance in arts had announced a decisive new perception of the fundamental relation between the Individual and Nature, or *Cosmos*: Religion's exclusive determination of Mankind's status in Nature gradually collapsed under the influence of the new discoveries and inventions of the natural sciences, and Religion alone could no longer indicate *the truths* of life or provide for any convincing explanations against the challenge from natural science. *The Earth was no longer a Divine creation, but a small and unimportant part of an endless universe and the picture of Man as having a determined place in Divine Cosmos could no longer be sustained.* Therefore, a new world-picture emerged which included a rediscovery of the ancient classic image of the *Individual* as master of reason and secular beauty, (hence the "renaissance"; one should not overlook, however, that the self-centred and aggressively outgoing subjectivity which was "rediscovered" in the 1750'es was entirely different from the ancient classic personification and harmonious unification of beauty and truth!). – But once the Individual had appeared as emancipated from religious normativity and was relieved from the task of deriving its identity from past elements outside itself, the development could not be halted; the *Classic Man* finally collapsed. *The breakthrough of Modernity* was further generated by the incipient industrialisation's dissolution of traditional life patterns, and finally emerged as the new model (paradigm) for perceiving the relation between Man and Nature; in philosophical terms, the autonomous *subject* was now constructed as the epistemological basis of rationality, and the fundamental distinctions between *subject and object, mind and body, belief and knowledge, emancipation and alienation*, etc., were irreversibly introduced. – This, however, created a serious loss of conceptual accountability; the Enlightment itself carried the fatal embryo of the legitimacy of fundamental disagreement and discourse about all social values, the *"Dialectics of Enlightment"*. The price for liberation of the individual subject was, in other words, an increasing – and crucial – *objectification and questionability of all human and social relations.*

Modernity and rationality

Giving up the fundamental historic ideals, however, left Modernity with the task of establishing its own new normativity of cultural clarification and self-reliance. Above all, the new principle of subjectivity demanded that civilisation exposed itself to *rational critics*, which in turn required a new conception of *rationality*: Reason is not acceptable if it cannot be critizised and satisfactorily accounted for.

Immanuel Kant was then among the first to suggest the division of *rationality* into three aspects, each with separate spheres of validity and explanatory force: a *theoretical* rationality (science), a *practical* rationality (law and ethics), and an *esthetic* rationality (arts). In doing so, it became possible to perceive *rationality* much more accurately and in the same time to subject this concept to criticism without the risk of a total

epistemological disaster. – Modernity's principle of subjectivity thus became a principle of *the right to critizise* – for the first time in history – the fundamental ideals and rationality of society *on a free and enlightened basis*. Perhaps this enterprise was overdone: mid-19th Century philosophy and intellectuals tended at least to question and critizise every possible aspect of historical and cultural phenomena, and "good rationality" simply came to imply a rigid scepticism and distance towards all social values – in the name of rationality itself.

This was the background for Nietzsche's *rejection of rationality* as the appropriate forum for social explanation and his consequential pointing at esthetic experience in the will for power. What Nietzsche favored was *not* nihilism, as he is often misunderstood to have done, but the revival of those (esthetic) parts of reason which had been excluded by the sceptic and valuelevelling approach in contemporary "rationality".

Perceptions of rationality

It is this tripartition of rationality and the question of designing a rational model for comprehending social values and cultural orientation which – still today – is disputed in *the crisis of Modernity*. Above all, *rationality* became the very center of rotation for every philosophical attempt to explain the true relations of nature and social life. Rationality may not be the perfect platform for this endeavour, but 200 years of philosophical discourse have not – so far – brought about any other and better suited point of orientation: some have strongly rejected the usefulness of rationality, while others hold it won't work without. But certainly, everyone relates to it.

One of our main problems in handling rationality is the *distinction between subject and object*, which was introduced above. The problem is, basically, that we have taught ourselves for centuries to perceive the world – from our individual and isolated positions – as something external and alien which is reflected in our mind through our consciousness and translated into mental pictures and ideas. Instinctively, we establish distanced and controlling relations to the matters in which we engage, so as to *objectivate* them in our skilful mastership things. Modern Western civilization's *perception of life* has adopted a purely objectivated and instrumental rationality in the sense that we selectively relate only, or at least mainly, to *technical* and *economical* aspects of societal development and human relations. We seek *right answers* to every question, as if an objective and verifiable truth could be identified in every detail. Our evaluation of social and human life is therefore reduced to assessments of technical or economical or otherwise quantifiable successes and failures. Accordingly, our strategy for actions to cope adequately with such events becomes instrumental as well.

No wonder that rationality has been subjected to strong criticism! *Postmodernist philosophy* has fiercely dismissed the explanatory potential of modern rationality values as they have appeared, for instance, in the last of the Big Doctrines at the end of the 19th Century: orthodox socialism and welfarestate liberalism. Neither of these theories – and the world pictures they present – can any longer explain the situation of today and motivate any progressive action. All values have now become common and accessible – and thereby indifferent. Postmodernist philosophers such as *Lyotard, Derrida, Baudrillard, Deleuze* a.o. hold in fact that no theory today can offer any commonly convincing and obliging set of values to serve as a point of cultural orientation in society. Western Culture, Lyotard argues, has lost its "Tales of Good and Bad" which ultimately used to legitimatize the policies. But anyway, since such Big Tales often carry the risk of turning into hegemonical thinking or totalitarian systems, we should rather learn to enjoy the present relief of idealistic dogmas and seek instead a new and critical rationality in the chaotic multitude of *free and individual* expressions of life. Modernity's original creation of the "subject" is thus out-dated, and the *rational subject* should be deconstructed. After all, our present free and democratic system has shown the best ability so far to improve the conditions of human life and to maintain and develop itself: *It needs no ideology.*

Habermas, on the other hand, turns himself against this total rejection of common rationality. First of all, he finds the postmodernist dismissal of modernity unnecessary and mistaken since it is founded exclusively in a one-sided focus onand *against the objective rationality*. But modernity, Habermas reminds, includes more than just the objective rationality. Building partly upon Kant's tripartition of rationality, Habermas suggests that modernity be understood so as to include three different worlds, each with their own type of rationality and legitimacy:

- the *objective*, external physical and biological world with its own particular *cognitive and instrumental rationality*;
- the *social* world with a particular *ethical and practical rationality*; and
- the *subjective*, internal and personal world with an *evaluative and esthetic rationality*.

When we discuss and assess the rationality of our modern culture, we must realise that it cannot – and shall not – be exclusively evaluated on the premises of the (first) "objective world". If we continue to do so, we shall fail to comprehend the *totality* of Modernity, the result of which is known to be a fatal submission to the coercive, cost-benefit oriented and instrumental rationality. Our wise evaluation of action rationality should, therefore, include both social and subjective

parameters as well, which effectively would improve the rationality potential of our decisions and norms. Habermas points to this effect at the necessity of the "free and unforced discourse" between competent parties as the ideal forum, in which all norms and actions can be evaluated and commonly accepted in their full, rational context; hence the theory of "*communicative action*" as a means to analyse and assess the rationality of the "life-world".

In the realm of *public authorities*, however, it seems as if the public system's own rationality cannot be evaluated correctly on the basis of "communicative action". This is due to the fact that the legislature, the administration and the judiciary are *not* primarily governed and reproduced by the rationality of the "unconstrained discourse", but rather by anonymous and independent agents such as Money, Power and Law. Accordingly, every single society should be assessed on the basis of both worlds, i.e. the *life-world* and the *system-world*. In the mutual relation between these two worlds, however, the rationality of the "system-world" has increasingly *colonised* the "life-world" to the effect that the free discourse between its actors is heavily biased or hampered by the self-sustaining and power-oriented logic of the "system-world". This fact must always be included in the assessment of life-world procedures.

The universal elements of the free discourse

It is Habermas' point that all *just norms* – in principle – must be understood as commanding products of the free and open discourse between competent parties. – Norms, in other words, are only *just* if and when they can be accepted – with their consequences and side-effects – by *all* through a collective process of choice without compulsion.

First of all, such norms can only be commonly accepted if all speech-actors are ready to *justify* their claims and norms by *arguments*, i.e. to persuade the others by coherent and convincing arguments that this claim or norm is really the best solution. In doing so, furthermore, they must declare and reveal their motives and intentions openly so as to facilitate access to the full test of every argument.

Secondly, all participants in the discourse must be willing to *subject themselves equally* to the same norms as those they wish to inflict upon others. Only if a norm or a claim can be accepted under these circumstances, it may surface as *just* and hence be transformed into justice.

Norms, on the other hand, which are unilaterally forced upon people under dictatorship or despotism, are not *just* norms, because the dictator cannot meet these obligations without revealing the irrationality of his position. It is these obligations which are *universal* to the "free and unforced" discourse – regardless of where we find ourselves in the world. What justice actually demands in a given social and historical context, however, cannot be decided in advance of a discourse of this kind. The *universal* elements in Habermas' concept of the "free and unforced discourse" are thus of a purely formal, not substantial, character; they relate to the *procedure* of the norm-making, but not to the *content* of justice.

This perception of *legitimacy* inevitably raises the question of *universality of legal norms:* can a legal norm ever be conceived with a universally acceptable content? In principle, this question should be answered in the negative, since every legal norm and every claim must always be determined and applied in its *local context*. A few points of amodification should be made, however:

First, international treaties are concluded freely between competent actors representing a number of states who – by their ratification – consent to transforming somehow the treaty norms into national law. In this case, of course, the treaty norms are applicable only in the ratifying states and are thus not *universal*. But at least these norms are not limited to a purely national context: identical legal norms are now, at least in principle, applicable within a multitude of states. One could maintain that in terms of the "free and unforced discourse", the necessary *given context* with regard to treaties is expanded to the territories of a number of states. An interesting observation, however, can be made at this point when we take a glance at the overall applicability of international treaties: The closer a treaty is associated with the traditional core of legal regulation, i.e. the protection of property and circulation of goods, services and capital, the more *extended* is it likely to become in its international applicability. Treaties on non-economical, humanitarian or politically controversial issues, on the other hand, are most often limited to particular *regions* and are not applicable beyond these.

Secondly, customary international law is said to be universally applicable – notably without the consent of states and other international legal subjects. In this case, I would argue that the few and simple rules of customary international law have emerged as norms of *good behaviour* in the common interest of all actors on the international level; norms, in otherwords, which are carried by evident, fair and convincing reasons. Although customary rules do not originate from any explicit communicative action, they may well be perceived as if this had been the case, since they are believed to express what all actors would be ready to accept anyhow in a free and unforced discourse. In whatever context a free discourse takes place, a certain frame needs to be established as the forum in which the arguments are exchanged. In the case of

customary international law, however, no such well-established frame or forum was available through the centuries when the customary rules were moulded, and this could perhaps explain and justify the lack of explicit agreement on the content of these particular norms. Alternatively, it could be argued that customary international law is indeed confirmed not only through the conduct of states, but also in the many international relations where these rules are referred to or advanced as justification of international claims. In this sense, customary international law would correspond to the category in domestic private law, which sometimes is referred to as *"Informal Law"*. In any case, we should be able to conclude that the *given context* here is expanded so as to encompass the entire international community, and that international law, as well as every other legal field or system, is *subject to the obligations of communicative action*.

"System-world" and "life-world" in an international legal context

I am, of course, well aware of the fact that customary international law is being largely criticized by many new countries as founded exclusively in the interests of Western industrialised states, and thus incapable of satisfying the needs of new countries, particularly in the Third World. The rational impact of this critique would probably have to be a serious, open and unforced discourse about every disputed rule of customary international law. As prudent as this would indeed be, the convening of an international conference on general customary law would seem preposterous, since customary law – by its very nature – can only be changed through alternated *patterns of action* among the interested actors, but not through *agreements* to this effect. – Instead, arguments about the rationality of customary rules are exchanged and assessed within confined areas and institutions such as, for instance, the *Law of the Sea* in the UN Conference on the Law of the Sea (UNCLOS III) and in the International Maritime Organisation (IMO), where customary rules are sometimes adjusted and transformed or codified into positive law.

But many states *are* indeed hesitant to initiate a review of norms in which they have a particular interest, or even to engage in the conception of new norms which ought to be accepted as just – despite a deviating practice. How do we explain such behaviour? – If we look at the reasons for their hesitance, the argument is most often made that adoption of new international norms in these areas would compromise the very principles of *sovereignty* and the right to *non-interference* in domestic matters. To what extent are we here facing a serious example of *the system-world's colonization of life-world rationality?* – Which kind of rational arguments can be advanced in defense of these principles, and how can they in turn be assessed and outweighed against other customary legal norms – in a free and unforced discourse? It goes far beyond the limits of this article to engage thoroughly in this discursive enterprise, but a few trends should at least be outlined at this point:

Both principles refer to *the State* as the rational and autonomous subject of international law which, in turn, implies a clear distinction between international and domestic law. This distinction, however, becomes difficult to maintain as the borderlines between international and national regulation are increasingly penetrated by the necessity of handling transnational actions and consequences in a mutually acceptable international framework. Today, a rapidly expanding number of legal areas are subject to detailed international regulation, bound to have decisive effects in Domestic Law through various constitutional procedures of immediate transformation or incorporation. Supported by the fast integration of national economies in the various *regions* of the world, an increasing number of legal standards are now commonly applicable within all States belonging to each region, *including certain customary norms.* If all Human Rights, for instance, cannot find distinct and *globally* acceptable interpretations, some of these rights at least are now believed to be invocable *with the same content* (or interpretation) in every State within a coherent international *region.* The classic concept of *the State*, in other words, appears to be badly jeopardised by modern political and economical evolution, and it is beyond doubt that supranational, regional institutions will henceforth succeed in many present state-functions vis à vis local municipal communities. Since the State-concept has had a tremendous influence on our entire perception of Law as basically limited to national territories, its gradual but indisputable dissolution is likely to bring about radical changes in future legal theory. In particular, these notions would seem to imply that:

- States are bound to *resign,* sooner or later, from their position as the *predominant international subject;* and that
- the tremendous importance which has been attached to the two principles of *sovereignty and non-intervention* as media for *system-world colonisation of i.a. Human Rights* will diminish.

Thus, the questions raised above regarding the rationality of state-hesitance to submitting to new standards in conflict with their established positions of interest, are really questions which strike to the very roots of international regulation. The same anonymous and indomitable agents as known from the national "system-world", notably *money and power,* seem to have the same colonising influence on the international level to the effect, that efforts to improve the international ethics and humanitarian standards are often frustrated. Money and power, one could say, have no limits.

The rationality of indigenous rights

As pointed out in the beginning of this article, the legal character of *Indigenous Rights* is disputed. A number of serious questions have been raised as to the *substance* of these rights: which particular rights and duties can be invoked in a legal context? – and to the *beneficiaries:* who exactly are entitled to invoke such claims – and for which forum? The uncertainty of these concerns is rooted partly in the objectivated rationality law, as described above, and partly in the system-world's rejection of anything that could be even thought of as subversive to the existing power structure of the states.

From the indigenous point of view, on the other hand, the matter is equally sacrosanct. The main concern here is the struggle against dissolution of their *cultures* caused by assimilation as well as pollution and dispossession of land for industrial purposes. Most states, I believe, have not denied per se the right of indigenous peoples to maintain their culture, but have been reluctant in providing for those remedies which are claimed in this respect by indigenous organisations, in particular the quest for political autonomy within their regions. Some countries have gone far to meet the demands while others have indeed been very restrictive, to say the least. Indigenous peoples in remote and geographically separated territories, like Greenland, seem to have been the most successful in their endeavours, subject to their level of political and industrial viability.

It would appear far too simple to say that we are dealing with a clash between, basically, culture and industrial expansion. Indigenous peoples, for one thing, are not only deeply engaged themselves in industrial enterprises, they are also to a large extent dependent on these activities and the welfare gained thereby.

If we apply some of the theoretical constructions developed earlier in this article in order to perceive the complexity in characterising and materialising indigenous rights, we should have competent indigenous and state representatives engaged in a "free and unforced discourse" about their relationship. The obligations of such discourse have been established above: each party would be compelled to advance their *rational* arguments fully and openly in this discourse so as to allow for a free and unprejudiced assessment of the better and the worse. The norms which would emerge as commonly acceptable from this "communicative action" could then be issued as "just" rules, ready for judicial support.

But what if we challenge the openness of the discourse and the equality of these two parties? Are they really exposing *all* their motives and are they *"equal"* in terms of a rational discourse? Even though government and aboriginal representatives may well be defined as "equal" in their capacity to bring forward the ultimate, rational values of their life-worlds in support of their case through the discourse, one cannot quite exclude the concern that governments – after all – are superior in their access to power, resources and information. And furthermore, the influence of the "system-world" is very likely entangled in the government positions, intentionally or not. For these reasons, I believe, one has to be careful in admitting the "freedom and unforcefulness" of this ongoing discourse. The experience of Canadian land claims negotiations, at least, show that huge government allocations to aboriginal organisations enabling them financially to buy the appropriate expertise, does not necessarily bring things in balance as long as the difference in perception of culture and values remains unrealised.

When it all comes down, it is exactly our ability to *perceive and accept differences* which is at stake in this complex situation. We may solve some of the most pertinent problems on a case-to-case basis, but we will irrevocably loose important parts of the entire cultural richness of human life, if the case of indigenous rights is not treated in a free and unprejudiced discourse including all sociological, anthropological, political and cultural estimations of the "life-world". For this fundamental reason, there can be no ways to argue against the treatment of indigenous rights in a legal context, both nationally and internationally.

The Authors

Mads Fægteborg, b. 1953, BA in eskimology. Runs a private consultant firm "Arctic Information". Author of books and several articles on Arctic military issues and environmental policy. Address: Arctic Information, Møntergade 16. DK-1116 København K. Denmark. Ph. (45) 33-13 02 92.

Frederik Harhoff, b. 1942, jurist LL.M. from the University of Copenhagen, 1977; currently Associate professor in International Law and EEC-Law with the Faculty of Law, University of Copenhagen, and Legal Adviser to the Greenland Home Rule Government. Address: Det retsvidenskabelige Institut, Københavns Universitet, Studiestræde 6, DK-1455 København K., Denmark. Ph. (45) 33-91 21 65, Fax: (45) 33-91 05 52.

Inge Kleivan, b. 1931, eskimologist. Associate professor, Institute of Eskimology, University of Copenhagen. Fieldwork in West Greenland. Publications on Inuit (primarily Greenlandic) culture and language. Address: Institute of Eskimology, Fiolstræde 10, DK-1171 Copenhagen K, Denmark. Ph. (45) 33-91 21 66.

Mark Nuttall, research fellow, Department of Social Anthropology, University of Edinburgh. Fieldwork in Upernavik district, northwest Greenland. Currently working on historical and cultural aspects of recent demographic changes in rural Scotland. Address: Department of Social Anthropology, University of Edinburgh, Adam Ferguson Building, George Square, Edinburgh EH8-9LL, Scotland. Ph. (44) 031-650-3845; Telex 72 74 42 UNIVEDG.

Robert Paine, anthropologist, Ph.D. Oxford. Major fieldwork among Norwegian Saami and many articles on this subject. Henrietta Harvey Professor of Anthropology, Memorial University of Newfoundland. Editor of ISER-Books, author of many articles in a variety of fields. Recent works: *The White Arctic* (1977), *Politically Speaking* (1981), *Advocacy and Anthropology* (1985). Address: Institute of Social and Economic Research, Memorial University of Newfoundland, St. John's, Newfoundland, A1C-5S7, Canada. Ph. 1-709-737-8156.

Robert Petersen, b. 1928, mag.art. in eskimology from University of Copenhagen. Professor of eskimology there 1975 and professor at Ilisimatusarfik from 1983/84. His scientific works include a broad range of linguistic, authropological and archaeological topics, mainly based on material from Greenland. Address: Ilisimatusarfik (Univ. of Greenland), 3900 Nuuk, Greenland. Ph. 299-24566, Fax. 299-24711.

Robert Phillipson, M.A. from Cambridge and Leeds Universities, England, Dr.phil. Amsterdam 1990. Taught English in Algeria and Yugoslavia. Since 1973 Associate Professor of English and Language Pedagogy, University of Roskilde, Denmark. Joint convenor, with Tove Skutnabb-Kangas, of the International Working Group on Linguistic Human Rights. Author, with Claus Faerch and Kirsten Haastrup of *Learner Language and Language Learning* (Multilingual Matters, 1984). Address: Roskilde University, Box 260, DK-4000 Roskilde, Denmark. Ph. (45) 46-75 77 11.

Tove Skutnabb-Kangas, Ph.D. Helsinki, Dr.phil. Roskilde, President of AILAs Scientific Commission on Language and Education in Multilingual Settings, Vice-president of International Sociology Association's Research Committee on Ethnic, Race and Minority Relations, is guest researcher at Roskilde University. Her latest books include *Minoritet, språk och rasism* 1986 (Minority, language and racism; Finnish translation Vähemmistö, kieli ja rasismi 1988) and *Minority Education: from Shame to Struggle* (edited with Jim Cummins, 1988). Address: see R. Phillipson.

Uffe Østergård, b. 1945, mag.art. in history, 1976 from Aarhus University. Associate professor there from 1976. Research fellow at the Centre for Cultural Research, AU, 1987-1992. Visiting research fellow at Harvard (USA) 1984-85 and 1988 and at Firenze EU. 1978-80. Many books and articles as author and editor published in English, French, German and the Scandinavian languages. Special fields of research: The Antiquity, Denmark in the 19th Century, authoritarian regimes of the 20th Century and the political culture of Italy, France, Austria-Hungaria, Germany, USA and the Nordic Countries. Address: (private) P. S. Krøyersvej 1, DK-8270 Højbjerg, Denmark Ph. (45) 86-27 56 01. Office: (45) 86-16 36 11. Fax. (45) 86-10 82 28.